UNIVERSITY OF NORTH CAROLINA AT CHAPEL HILL
DEPARTMENT OF ROMANCE LANGUAGES

NORTH CAROLINA STUDIES
IN THE ROMANCE LANGUAGES AND LITERATURES

Founder: URBAN TIGNER HOLMES

Editor: CAROL L. SHERMAN

D1706235

Distributed by:

UNIVERSITY OF NORTH CAROLINA PRESS

CHAPEL HILL
North Carolina 27515-2288
U.S.A.

NORTH CAROLINA STUDIES IN THE
ROMANCE LANGUAGES AND LITERATURES
Number 261

A MEDIEVAL PILGRIM'S COMPANION

A MEDIEVAL PILGRIM'S COMPANION

Reassessing
El libro de los huéspedes
(Escorial MS. h.I.13)

BY

THOMAS D. SPACCARELLI

CHAPEL HILL

NORTH CAROLINA STUDIES IN THE ROMANCE
LANGUAGES AND LITERATURES
U.N.C. DEPARTMENT OF ROMANCE LANGUAGES

1998

Library of Congress Cataloging-in-Publication Data

Spaccarelli, Thomas Dean, 1947-
   A medieval pilgrim's companion: reassessing El libro de los huéspedes (Escorial MS. h.I.13) / by Thomas D. Spaccarelli.
      p. – cm. – (North Carolina studies in the Romance languages & literatures; no. 261).
   Includes bibliographical references.
   ISBN 0-8078-9265-3 (pbk.)
      1. Escorial. Real Biblioteca. Manuscript. H-I-13. 2. Christian saints – Legends – History and criticism. 3. Legends, Christian – Spain – History and criticism. 4. Spanish literature – To 1500 – History and criticism 5. Christian pilgrims and pilgrimages – Spain – Santiago de Compostela.   I. Title.   II. Series.

BX4662.S68   1999
270'.092'2 –dc21

98-35344
CIP

This book is published with the generous support of the University of the South and with a subvention from the Program for Cultural Cooperation between Spain's Ministry of Education and Culture and United States' Universities.

Cover: original drawing by Adam W. Carlos, based on "The Seven Works of Charity" by the Master of Alkmaar.

Cover design: Shelley Gruendler

ISBN 0-8078-9265-3

IMPRESO EN ESPAÑA

PRINTED IN SPAIN

DEPÓSITO LEGAL: V. 815 - 1999

ARTES GRÁFICAS SOLER, S. L. - LA OLIVERETA, 28 - 46018 VALENCIA

TABLE OF CONTENTS

To my teachers, with gratitude and admiration:

Lucille Braun
James Compton
† Ruth El Saffar
Jerry Rank

ACKNOWLEDGMENTS

This study and my earlier edition of the *Libro de los huéspedes* (henceforth *LH*) have taken nourishment from various sources that should be acknowledged from the outset. My temerity in proposing the unity of the *LH* and in breaking with the traditional ways of seeing h.I.13 has found sustenance and encouragement in John Dagenais' *The Ethics of Reading in Manuscript Culture.* In particular, his argument against the importance that critical editions (i.e. "coherent texts") have assumed in our profession, his respect for scripta as we find them, and his concept of *lecturature* are all reflected in the comments I make concerning the *LH* and in the ways I perceive the text. [1]

Jonathan Sumption's monumental work, *Pilgrimage: An Image of Mediaeval Religion*, is a companion to all who concern themselves with the history, reality, and lore concerning the theme as is the three volume *Las peregrinaciones a Santiago de Compostela* by Luis Vázquez de Parga *et al.* My understanding of pilgrimage liter-

---

[1] I am aware of the fact that Dagenais himself has proposed that we drop fictions such as the title *Libro de buen amor* for more concrete entities such as Salamanca, Biblioteca Universitaria, MS 2663 (MS S). He does so, of course, because the text generally studied as the *Libro de buen amor* is a philological construction that never existed in the Middle Ages. As he states it in "Bothersome Residue": "To put all this another way, MSS S, G, and T are medieval books, the *Libro de buen amor* is not" (253). In the case of a canonical text such as the *LBA*, the text we know is what Dagenais calls a "flight from presence" (249). It would seem, then, that my giving a title to h.I.13 works against the proposals of Dagenais. On the contrary, I give a name to the codex so that for the first time it will be observed, read, and analyzed as a physical entity and presence from the Middle Ages without being fragmented as has been the case up until now.

ature and the tradition of the "Gregorian pattern of pilgrimage" is a result of reading F. C. Gardiner's *The Pilgrimage of Desire*. William Melczer's loosely defined concept of "romanesque-form culture" in his translation and study of *The Pilgrim's Guide* has also served as a unique source of inspiration. My interpretation of the *LH* will show how it too was informed by and became part of this romanesque-form culture or what Stephen G. Nichols, Jr. calls in *Romanesque Signs* the Road's "semiotic system." Nichols has also inspired my comments on *Imitatio Christi*.

From Brian Stock's *The Implications of Literacy* I take the concept of "textual communities." Although his concept is transformed in my study, Stock's ideas have been essential to my understanding of how the *LH* might have been read by medieval people themselves. Michael Camille's insistence that we restore the sumptuousness of medieval reading has guided much of my work on the *LH*. María Rosa Menocal's example of synchronic reading in *Shards of Love* and her insistence on the cacophony of the Spanish Middle Ages encourage me in my participatory reading of the *LH*.

Professor Antonio Momplet of Madrid's Complutense University, and my cohort in so many activities concerning the Road to Santiago, has taught me to "read" medieval art. His influence on how I see the pilgrimage is so profound that it would be difficult to tell where his influence stops. My dear friend and fellow pilgrim, Jack Hitt, has shared his wisdom, enthusiasm, and good humor concerning the Road over the course of a twenty-year friendship. I would mention Jack's book, *Off the Road*, as one of my inspirations, but to limit Jack's influence to that of one book would diminish the importance he holds in my heart and mind. John Maier joined me in earlier excursions through the folios of the *LH* and his companionship continues in spirit to this day. Brian Dutton was the first person to tell me of the existence of h.I.13, and it is he who suggested that I could find a lifetime's worth of work in its folios. He was right, as usual.

In what seems a lifetime ago, Lloyd Kasten shared with me his joy in dealing with medieval manuscripts in his masterful classes on paleography and textual criticism. If readers of this study perceive the joy with which it has been produced, they should know that its origin is to be found around that glowing, heavy table in the Seminary in Madison. Ruth El Saffar touched my life and work in so many ways that it would be hard to enumerate them. Ruth exemplified how the passions and concerns of one's work could be integrated with those of everyday life. She taught that literature can and does have impact on individuals, peoples, and nations in both positive and negative ways. She taught and embodied the ethics of reading Spanish literature decades before the concept became current in our profession. It is my hope that this study and my earlier edition honor the learning and friendship that these two superb Hispanists shared with me.

Fehl Cannon and Thompson Yee, both of the Library of Congress, aided me in countless ways, always showing patience for what seemed like a sustained lunacy. Their generosity – the embodiment of guest/host theology – will never be forgotten. Alda Blanco, soulmate and friend, has opened her home and heart to me in Madrid and in Madison – my debt to her is enormous. Cristina González, Steve Raulston, and Joe Snow all read portions of an earlier version of this study and through their challenges and suggestions the final version has been infinitely improved. Let me record here my gratitude for their time and professionalism. Ivy Corfis not only made valuable suggestions to an early version of this study, but she generously shared with me her computational expertise and her precious time throughout its preparation. I am most grateful. The errors that remain, and my stubborn insistence on certain ideas, cannot be attributed to these friends and colleagues.

Tammy Scissom, Sondra Bridges, and Sherry Cardwell of the Office of Print Services of The University of the South provided computer wizardry and patience through innumerable printings, format changes, etc. I record here my gratitude and debt to their knowledge and kindness. The Research Grants Committee of The University of the South provided funds that allowed me to make a final consultation of h.I.13 at El Escorial late in 1995. The Committee's generosity is most appreciated. Finally, the dedication of this book records a debt of gratitude to my undergraduate professors whose excellence and professionalism encourage me to this day.

CHAPTER I

INTRODUCTORY REMARKS

> ". . . Las luengas peregrinaciones
> hacen a los hombres discretos . . ."
>
> Miguel de Cervantes, *El licenciado Vidriera*

The codex traditionally known as Ms. h.I.13 of El Escorial, which I have named the *Libro de los huéspedes,* has generally been edited by medievalists as nine separate works:[1]

> De Santa Maria Madalena
>
> De Santa Marta
>
> La estoria de Santa Maria Egiçiaca
>
> De Santa Cataljna
>
> De vn cauallero Plaçidas que fue despues cristiano & ouo nonbre Eustaçio
>
> La estoria del rey Gujllelme
>
> El cuento muy fermoso del enperador Otas de Roma & de la infante Florençia su fija & del buen cauallero Esmero
>
> Vn muy fermoso cuento de una santa enperatris que ouo en Rroma & de su castidat
>
> Vn noble cuento del enperador Carlos Maynes de Roma & de la buena enperatris Seuilla su mugier

This now traditional fragmentation of the codex has resulted in our failure to perceive that the book was compiled and comprehended in its own time as a unified work. Modern editions of the

---

[1] See List of Works Cited for a comprehensive index of the various editions of the *LH.*

separate chapters, produced in the tradition of scholarly concepts such as source texts, regularization of language, literary genres, the primacy of the relationship author/work, etc., have diminished our ability to comprehend the unique and unified nature of the *LH*, thereby distorting our knowledge and appreciation of the canon of medieval Spanish literature.[2] I intend to show in this study that the *LH* is a text intimately related to the pilgrimage to Santiago de Compostela and to various religious, literary, and artistic traditions associated with it. To restore the integrity of this text, I believe, is also to provide a more historically accurate view of medieval Spanish culture and of the concerns and issues that fired the enthusiasm of medieval people.

My contention is that the nine texts that make up the *LH*, texts usually seen as independent works with their own histories, sources, traditions of commentary and criticism, and, indeed, their own distinct genres, were translated, compiled, and anthologized with the goal of producing a single book whose purpose was to provide edification, encouragement, and entertainment to groups of pilgrims on their way to the sanctuary of St. James in Compostela. The team of compilers produced a work in which the pilgrim readers and hearers[3] would be presented with numerous characters, situations, descriptions, and themes in which they as pilgrims saw themselves reflected. I believe the compilers were guided by specific religious and social ideas which they hoped to propagate far and

---

[2] In our 1982 article "MS. Escurialense . . ." John Maier and I indicated the evidence that exists to establish h.I.13 as a unified "anthology." Most subsequent work on the texts has made reference to that notion – see, for instance, Walsh/Thompson, "Myth"; González, "Otas" and "Vna santa"; Spaccarelli, "Recovering." Some of the texts have traditionally been studied together. The lives of Mary and Martha, for instance, have usually been edited and studied in unison probably because the two were sisters and because the works refer to one another. The *Plácidas* text and the *Rey Gujllelme* likewise have been studied together because of the great similarities between the texts – see, for instance, the introduction to Maier's edition of the *Rey Gujllelme,* and Liffen.

[3] I shall assume for the purposes of this study that the *LH* was intended to be read aloud to groups of pilgrims of various levels of literacy. There are a number of studies that bear upon the topic of the delivery of medieval literature and on the issues of orality and textuality. The interested reader is referred to the studies of Cazelles (*Lady* . . . 13), Dagenais *Ethics*, Stock *Implications* and "Medieval Literacy," Walker "Oral Delivery," Vitz, Zumthor and Volume 16, no. 1 (1984) of *New Literary History* dedicated to "Oral and Written Traditions in the Middle Ages." See also below, section IV.B, "Santa Maria Egiçiaca: pilgrims, art, and equality."

wide by means of the influence their book would have on pilgrims. This ideology has social and political facets as well as literary and artistic ones. In this sense, it is possible that the *LH* was compiled in order to foster the creation of what Brian Stock in *The Implications of Literacy* has called a "textual community."[4] In addition, I believe the *LH* is a Spanish example of what Sheila Delany has called an "evolution toward coherency: a group of short pieces incorporated at some point within a broader structural framework" (xxi). If the *LH* originated in this way, it would be an excellent example of the way John Dagenais claims medieval literature happens:

> I began to see that it is at the edges of manuscripts and in the various activities by which medieval people transformed one manuscript into another – commentary, *translation*, adaptation, reworking, and the "mechanical" act of copying – that the most important part of "medieval literature" happens. (*Ethics*, xvi) [my emphasis]

In addition, it would reflect well his concept of reading as an ethical activity:

> Texts were acts of demonstrative rhetoric that reached out and grabbed the reader, involved him or her in praise and blame, in judgments about effective and ineffective human behavior. They engaged the reader, not so much in the unravelling of meaning as in a series of ethical meditations and of personal ethical choices. They required the reader to take a stand about what he or she read. (*Ethics*, xvii)[5]

Evelyn Birge Vitz speaks in a similar vein about medieval hagiography:

---

[4] One might note that the examples of such communities presented by Stock are "heretical communities," (88 ff.) and were met with various forms of suppression in the Middle Ages. His definition of such communities is at p. 90. Note also the affirmation of Gerhart B. Ladner in *"Homo Viator"*: "These pilgrimages – though at times they led to outright disorder – were not only an expression of spiritual fervor, but also an occasion for contact between different social and ethnical groups and for human experiences of all kinds" (245).

[5] Also see *Ethics*, p. 61 last paragraph.

Those old stories that jongleurs sang and monks read aloud were not completely true (some of them were not true at all). But they provided more than just entertainment and pleasure to a largely nonliterate, nonreading public: these stories *spoke* to people, inspiring many to a leap of faith, to a new life. (113)

CHAPTER II

THE QUESTION OF UNITY IN THE *LH*

In our article "MS. Escurialense . . . ," John Maier and I contended that the *LH* was "a highly organized anthology of tales which were collected and ordered (and probably translated) with several specific criteria in mind" (20). Several scholars had earlier searched for a unifying principle that could be applied to the *LH*. There were two general approaches to their suggestions. The first, which has some validity, is the fact that so many of the tales involve female protagonists. [1] This idea was espoused by Amador de los Ríos in the nineteenth century and found favor with Walker (*Egiçiaca*, xx-xxi; "From French Verse" 241), and was repeated in our "MS. Escurialense . . ." (20). Michel, on the other hand, saw Amador's error in thinking that the book belonged to the library of Isabel the Catholic and that it was the *Flos Sanctorum* mentioned in the inventory of the monarch's library. On the contrary, she (ci), followed by Walsh and Thompson (21) and Rees Smith (xvii), believed that the codex was meant as a diversion for weary pilgrims on the Road to Santiago. She states:

---

[1] Female protagonists and female issues are important to the unity of the book, but in ways that are quite distinct from those generally discussed in the literature. See below, section IV.C, "De santa cataljna . . . making the case for women." It is worth contemplating the *LH* as a type of female legendary along the lines suggested by Sheila Delany for Osbern Bokenham's *Legends of Holy Women*:

> The Austin friar gives us not only an all-female hagiography . . . but a gallery of powerful, articulate women who are indubitably worthy to do God's work. Some of them are well educated; some give sound political advice to a monarch; some preach, converting hundreds and thousands to Christianity; some walk on water or perform resurrection. (xxx)

The pilgrim movement to Santiago was at its height in the fourteenth century. Every important pilgrim group had its jongleur whose duty it was to break the monotony of the way or of the long evenings at the hospices. And if not the jongleur, perhaps a monk of the hospice served as entertainer at evening . . . and read to the pilgrims legends of the saints and other edifying tales, that lent a special interest because they savored of an experience similar to that of the listeners. Such may have been the purpose of our MS, a volume for Spanish pilgrims, with stories of favorite saints of the epoch – as SS. Mary Magdalene and Martha, hostesses of Our Lord; St. Catherine, one of the fourteen Helpers in Need; St. Mary of Egypt, whose life would inspire hope of salvation into the most degraded of human beings – and its tales of virtuous men and women whose lives of abnegation and patient endurance – often of trials borne while exiled from their native land – served as encouragement as well as entertainment for the medieval traveler. (lxxv-lxxvi)

It is my belief that Michel was correct in her assessment, but she did not go far enough in her appreciation of the importance the book gives to pilgrims and pilgrimage as pivotal characters and images and as central reference points. Consequently she failed to see the book as the unified whole that it is. Indeed, I believe there is more than ample evidence to show that the *LH* is a vernacular Book of Saint James that parallels in every way the following statement of Stephen G. Nichols, Jr. concerning the better known but less useful[2] Latin *Liber Sancti Jacobi*:

---

[2] By "less useful" I mean that for the average pilgrim to Santiago in the Middle Ages any book in the vernacular, everyday tongue was immediately more useful than a book in Latin. This is not to say that a book in Latin might not be of higher quality in terms of intellectual and scholarly content; rather it is a simple statement of fact that most people find their mother tongues more useful than what might be at best the "half-understood symbols" (33) of a foreign tongue mentioned by Michael Camille in "Seeing and Reading." As he has stated it: "Latin had an aura as it was separated from the baser speech acts of everyday existence in the complex rituals of a clerical group, whose monopoly was the manipulation of this metalanguage" (30). One might also consider Rita Copeland's statement in *Rhetoric, Hermeneutics, and Translation*: "Real power lies, not in status, but in effective, persuasive communication, and here the vernacular is clearly in charge" (183). I would offer as contemporary evidence the fact that the current revival of interest in *The Pilgrim's Guide* among scholars of the Middle Ages and the Road to Santiago is directly related to the fact that there are several good translations of the Latin text available in Spanish, English, and other European languages (for a listing of these translations see Shaver-Crandell and Gerson 64). If this can be said of a group of

The pilgrimage was, as Bédier has long since demonstrated, a so-cial, economic, and cultural phenomenon, as well as a religious one. It served as a stimulus for artistic works of various kinds and facilitated their circulation. The primary text which we possess today describing the pilgrimage to Compostela as a semiotic system, as a network of expressive forms–texts, monuments, sites – is the Guide de Pèlerin de Sainte-Jacques de Compostelle. (c. 1130-40) (151)

The Guide to Santiago and the various gazetteers provided by contemporary scholars are aimed at teaching pilgrims about the religious, historic, artistic, and culinary marvels of the road while warning them of its pitfalls and dangers. The *LH*, on the other hand, is aimed at taking that very knowledge (which every pilgrim would have gained through daily experience) and using it as part of a larger project of building and fortifying the pilgrim guest/host community.

Let us ponder in which ways the *LH* might be construed as a vernacular Book of St. James, especially with reference to the structural elements, framework, or semiotic system to be discussed below.

---

well-educated, twentieth-century medievalists, presumably trained in Latin, at the very least the same can be said for the hoi polloi of medieval Spain. It is worth noting at this point that Shaver-Crandell and Gerson (56) doubt that the *Guide* was ever carried on the road by pilgrims.

CHAPTER III

STRUCTURAL FRAMEWORK

In order to ascertain the structure given the book by its compilers, I propose to look at the following elements: (A) Biblical passages that define pilgrimage; (B) The "Gregorian pattern of pilgrimage" as set forth by F. C. Gardiner; (C) Guest/host theology; (D) Traditions of the pilgrimage to Santiago; (E) Iconographical aspects of art on the pilgrimage route; (F) The notion of *Imitatio Christi* (G) The theme of egalitarianism; (H) The matter of misogyny and feminism; and (I) The pattern of family separation, wandering, and travails. First I shall describe the various elements mentioned, showing either how they define pilgrimage and pilgrims as understood in the Middle Ages or at least how they bear upon the topic. Next I shall look at the text of the *LH*, showing in what ways it contains these elements and utilizes them to define and propagate its vision of spirituality and society. In this way I shall respond to the reservations of María Morrás expressed in her review of Rees Smith's edition of the lives of Mary and Martha. She notes his assertion that the codex was intended as a diversion to be read aloud to groups of pilgrims: "Aunque la suposición es más que razonable, se echa en falta un análisis, siquiera somero, del estilo y de la estructura narrativa en que se aíslen aquellos rasgos que pudieran apoyar tal tesis" (116). The present study provides exactly the analysis envisioned by Morrás.

If it can be shown that these elements are present in the text and that one, they cohere in such a way as to give it various levels of significance and meaning while two, they provide the readers and hearers with material for contemplation concerning their own spiritual life and society, then my assertions concerning the compilers, their intentions, and the unity of the book will meet what Gardiner calls the "mutual relevancy" test: "The more central a theme is to be, the more parts of a text it must make mutually relevant" (4). It is true that the presence of any single one of these elements would not necessarily relate the book to pilgrims and pilgrimage. On the other hand, the consistent convergence of these elements in various patterns throughout the work confirm as operative the connection I propose.

Since I shall make constant reference to the compilers and to the concept of a pilgrim community of readers and hearers it is appropriate at this point to elaborate what I mean by those terms. I believe the collection was the result of a conscious effort on the part of a group of compilers to provide a unified body of texts that would serve to entertain, teach, and encourage groups of Spanish-speaking pilgrims en route to Santiago de Compostela. The compilers chose the texts they desired to translate, used French versions of the tales for the most part as their sources (sometimes also using Latin versions when available), and utilized as their intermediate language Galician, as per the statement on fol. 99d (*De vna santa enperatris*): "uos quiero retraer fermosos miraglos asy como de latin fue trasladado en frances e de frances en gallego."[1] They ordered the tales in such a way that when read in sequence they would present and develop themes, ideas, and images that would appeal to their pilgrim readers and hearers. The compilers were either monks or nuns working in Galicia.

The compilers intended their work to be disseminated by means of oral reading in the monasteries, hospitals and refuges built and maintained for pilgrims along the main pilgrimage routes.[2] For this

---

[1] Traditional approaches to the texts of h.I.13 accept this statement for the *Santa enperatris* text alone. In any given edition there is usually no mention of the contents of the other texts of the codex. If my hypothesis concerning the unity of the collection is true, then a Galician intermediate version would have existed for all the tales of the collection and such a version would explain most of the linguistic curiosities to be found in the tales. In fact, such is the case, as will be shown below.

[2] Baukje Finet-van der Schaaf, making reference to the *Carlos Maynes* text and its sixteenth-century printed version the *Hystoria de la Reyna Sebilla* only, insists that they were intended for oral delivery: "La *Hystoria* paraît, comme *El Cuento*, destinée à être lue devant un auditoire . . ." (36). The Dutch scholar then cites P. Chaunu for evidence concerning her view. The case in point deals with the reading of romances in the Americas during the Spanish Empire: "D'après P. Chaunu, les romans de chevalerie espagnols furent effectivement lus à haute voix dans le milieu des *conquistadores* au Mexique" (*ibid.*).

purpose they could have prepared more than one copy of their text themselves or urged it to be copied by other institutions. One can envision the monks of a master house propagating the text to its affiliated institutions. As an example, one thinks of the Benedictine monastery at Sahagún which, according to the *Diccionario de historia eclesiástica de España*, "poseía más de 130 filiaciones" such that one could speak of the "ordo Sancti Facundi" (III, 1675). Cluny provides an example of the kind of network of affiliated monasteries that I have in mind when I speak of this kind of dissemination. Concerning these monastic networks, Pérez de Urbel states:

> Indudablemente, el torrente de la peregrinación permitía vivir con la práctica de todos los servicios del hospedaje a los monasterios situados en las cercanías del camino francés. Cluny se dio cuenta de ello, y no dejó de manifestar un vivo interés en poseer una cadena de filiaciones a lo largo de la ruta, lo mismo en Francia que en España; y conseguido este primer objeto, puso al servicio de los peregrinos todo su instinto de organización, esforzándose por rodearles de todas las facilidades que entonces se podían alcanzar, y desplegando su poderosa influencia para acrecentar aquel movimiento internacional, llamado a producir tantos frutos de renovación religiosa y de progreso en todos los órdenes de la cultura. (*El monasterio* 149)

John K. Walsh has made a similar conjecture in "Relic and Literature," but posits Astorga as the place of composition. Walsh's contention corroborates my own:

> My hypothesis is that the orb of Astorga . . . was precisely the place where the texts of French romances and saints' tales (the brand of hagiography akin to and intertwined with adventure romances) were often translated or reworked in Castilian. In the first place, of course, the fourteenth-century collection of five hagiographic tales . . . and four romances . . . in MS h-I-13 of the Escorial is from this region. (15)

It is possible, however, that the deteriorated, even mutilated, state of h.I.13 is a result of having been carried along the pilgrimage route.[3] It is marked by heavy use (worn pages, tears, etc.) and some

---

[3] For a detailed description of the manuscript see Maier/Spaccarelli, 18-20 and Walsh/Thompson, 18-21 and the bibliographic citations in both studies.

of its folios have been described as "wrinkled and water damaged" (Spaccarelli, "Recovering"), although perhaps *weather damaged* might be a more accurate description if such a scenario of portability were true. Whatever the case may be, one can state unequivocally that MS h.I.13 is not a luxury codex–its purpose was to be read, not to serve as an awe-inspiring object of ceremony.

Vázquez de Parga provides the following description of the routine of services provided to pilgrims at the pilgrims' hospital at Roncesvalles. Note that it includes reading to the pilgrims in what I assume would have been refectory style, exactly the situation I envision for the *LH*.

> Aquellos que eran servidos por alguna comunidad, como los de Roncesvalles y Burgos, debían mantener un culto ajustado a las horas canónicas de carácter conventual. En Roncesvalles había diez hermanos 'residentes in claustro' y ocho diáconos, subdiáconos y acólitos, aparte de los oficiales como el subprior, el celario, el sacristán, el enfermero y otros. Cuatro sacerdotes seculares, que fuesen bien instruidos en el canto y la lectura, tenían a su cargo el bautizar en el hospital, predicar cuando fuese necesario, confesar, dar la comunión, enterrar a los muertos e '*in mensa legere peregrinis*'. (I, 341) [my emphasis]

I see no reason whatsoever to assume that the routine of hospitality elsewhere was any different. If the readings were to be successful, they would need to have been done by skilled performers ("bien instruidos en el canto y la lectura"). Scholarship has shown that it was typical of the *LH* translations to pare down their French sources (see below, chapter V), nevertheless the abbreviated texts exhibit sufficient dialogue, drama, variety of characters and voices, and enough rich description to merit more than a monotone, especially if the reader/performer intended to draw and maintain the listener's attention.

When I speak of the pilgrim community of readers and hearers I assume it to be made up of groups of Spanish pilgrims of all walks of life and educational levels, although I envision the majority to be unlettered. It may be that some had letters, even Latin, but by and large I agree with Keith Whinnom's assertion that "Medieval literature in Spanish is, *ipso facto*, literature for illiterates . . ." (11). The community I posit is made up of women and men, and, in fact, the role and status of women are among the central concerns of the work. Jonathan Sumption points out the following information concerning female pilgrims:

> For most of the middle ages, however, women were not particularly noted as pilgrims. So much so that the sudden reappearance of large numbers of female pilgrims in the fourteenth and fifteenth centuries called for comment, usually hostile comment. (261-262)

This is exactly the period when the *LH* would have sought its audience. Cristina González has actually suggested that the *LH* was intended as recruitment propaganda for nuns ("*Vna santa enperatris*" 165), a genial idea that is not essentially at odds with my concept of a pilgrim community. Marta González Vázquez has studied the presence of females on the Camino in the Middle Ages and provides a bounty of information concerning all aspects of their activities both as guests and hostesses (i. e. as pilgrims and caregivers).

The pilgrim community of the *LH* would be an egalitarian community made up of women and men of many social classes. The book argues forcefully for a spirituality that John Dominic Crossan calls egalitarian commensality and itinerant radicalism (*Historical Jesus* 341-348) and for a theology of community and presence over one of authority and proof (*Historical Jesus* 396-404; see also section A, B, and C immediately below). The book seeks to elicit a positive response from this community to its mildly anti-clerical and anti-royal ideology (in this it parallels certain aspects of the ethos Colin Smith has noted in the *romancero tradicional*–see Smith 13-15). Where Brian Stock has talked of heretical "textual communities" (*Implications* 88 ff.) I believe we might better speak of the *LH* as fostering a *heterodox* community of pilgrims and hosts that has much in common with primitive Christianity.

After describing the theoretical framework that will be used in my analysis of the work, I shall look at the constituent tales of the *LH* in order, elaborating in each case more details concerning the compilers, their work, and the community of readers and hearers.

A. Biblical Texts

Pilgrimage is a largely misunderstood phenomenon. Typically it is seen as an archetypical voyage of discovery towards a final destination or shrine often endowed with enormous symbolic value. Medieval Christianity coupled to this view the idea that the voyage was an imitation of Christ depicted as the stranger, unrecognized by his disciples as he walked to Emmaus. In its earliest manifestations, pilgrimage was more a rejection of the world and of civilization than a trip to any specific place. One text quoted by Sumption states: "be exiles for God's sake, and go not only to Jerusalem but everywhere, for God himself is everywhere" (96). The medieval understanding of pilgrimage was informed by countless biblical references, but four in particular stand out:[4]

1) Luke 24: 13-35–the Emmaus tale. The Emmaus tale deals with the appearance of the risen Christ to two of the disciples as they were journeying to Emmaus from Jerusalem. In Luke's version, one is identified as Cleopas and the other is left unidentified. The medieval tradition identified that second disciple as Luke himself. The disciples did not recognize Jesus, the "stranger" (in the Vulgate version "peregrinus"), when they came upon him on the road. They had been discussing the events of recent days and tell the stranger of those events indicating their own doubts as to the resurrection of Christ. The "stranger" then goes about lecturing them on how those events respond to the prophecies of the scriptures, beginning with Moses. When the group arrives at Emmaus, the disciples press hospitality upon the stranger, and when he accepts and breaks bread with them they recognize him as their risen Lord. They rush back to Jerusalem to report on this "appearance" and remark at how although they had not recognized him during their conversation on the road, their hearts had burned within their breasts upon hearing his words. There are many ways to interpret this story. A focus on Christ will result in a story whose purpose is to provide yet another piece of evidence concerning the resurrection. A focus on the disciples and on the readers provides an interpretation that insists on the continual presence of Christ whenever hospitality is of-

---

[4] For more details concerning biblical references and allusions see Holloway, Chapters 1 and 2.

fered to a stranger. This second interpretation stresses the sacred nature of hospitality and its connection to the continuing presence of the living Christ.[5] Finally, as Julia Bolton Holloway points out, "The Emmaus tale was linked to pilgrimage because Luke's Gospel text had Cleopas term Christ 'peregrinus,' 'stranger,' or, as it was understood in the Middle Ages, 'pilgrim'" (20).

2) Hebrews 11: 13-16 – Christians are strangers, passing travellers looking for their heavenly home (in Latin, *patria*). The text gives examples of biblical figures (Abel, Enoch, Noah, Abraham, Sarah) who were paragons of faith, who knew that there is "a better country" to come. This is the source of Gregory's *patria* (see section B, below).

3) Hebrews 13: 1-2 – Welcome strangers, they might be angels. This is a call to love one's brothers and sisters and a reminder that some have given hospice to stangers only to find out later that they were angels.

4) Matthew 25: 31-46 – In the Last Judgment humans will be divided into two groups: the saved, called sheep (those who fed, clothed and took in Christ as stranger), and the damned, called goats (those who did not), who will burn in "eternal fire." The text reminds Christians that fulfilling the works of charity, especially that of giving hospice and aid to the most humble of Christ's followers, is doing so to him. This passage is the source text for the typical image of the *Christus Pantocrator* or Christ-in-majesty that is depicted in so many of the tympanums of medieval church portals. It is also one of the sources of the remarkable panel, "The Seven Works of Charity" by the Master of Alkmaar now housed in Amsterdam's Rijksmuseum dated at 1504. The panel consists of seven scenes, each depicting one of the seven acts of charity: feeding the hungry; giving drink to the thirsty; clothing the naked; burying the dead; giving hospice to pilgrims (strangers); visiting the sick; and comforting prisoners. The central scene, the burial of the dead, also represents a Christ-in-majesty judging the dead at their resurrections. The scene of giving hospice to pilgrims depicts the pilgrims in traditional garb adorned with the scallop emblem of Santiago. In

---

[5] This passage can be related to the themes of open commensality and radical egalitarianism (including women), and to a theology of presence over one of proof. See the arguments of biblical scholar John Dominic Crossan in *Historical Jesus* 261-264 and 398-404 and the more popularized *Jesus* 66-70 and 170-181.

all the scenes an inconspicuous Christ, obviously the same figure as the Christ-in-majesty, is shown within the group of these, the least of his servants. The panel is illustrative also of the "Gregorian pattern of pilgrimage" and of guest/host theology (see B and C immediately below).

There are many other biblical references that can be construed to deal with pilgrimage. The Exodus tale, for instance, can be seen as a forty-year pilgrimage to the "patria." I have merely listed here four that I consider fundamental to the medieval phenomenon.

B. The "Gregorian Pattern of Pilgrimage"

In *The Pilgrimage of Desire* F. C. Gardiner has shown that in the medieval Latin world the Emmaus tale was understood as the quintessential pilgrimage story. As a preliminary to studying the medieval pilgrim plays he does an analysis of Pope Gregory the Great's commentaries on Luke's Emmaus tale and of a cluster of concepts and words[6] dealing with pilgrimage and what he calls "pilgrim people – *populus peregrinus*." First, the pilgrim lives in a state of desire for the fatherland (*patria*) (cf. Hebrews ll: 13-16), for "unlike the angels, the pilgrim lives as an exile, knowing and hoping he has a fatherland, yet without a sight of that celestial home" (17). Obviously, from the Christian perspective, this is the condition of all human beings in this world. This situation of desire is a source of anxiety, pain, and travail for the pilgrim. However, various signs, ceremonies, and experiences are available by which humans can approach the fatherland since for the *populus peregrinus*, "time intersects with eternity, and . . . man does encounter deity along the journey – that is, . . . the human exile finds the celestial home in men and their words . . ." (19) in the act of being a *hospes* ("host" – see below, "Guest/Host Theology"). In the Gregorian commentaries, "The stranger is literally identified as deity" and "the union of friends" is seen "as a pilgrim-experience" (54). Gardiner points out that for Gregory, the two disciples are not totally separated

---

[6] For the Gregorian pattern the cluster of words includes: desire, love, exile, men, works, pilgrim, pilgrimage, hardship, celestial fatherland. The cluster of words we will study in association with the *LH* will overlap but be distinct from the "Gregorian pattern."

from Christ for "Doubt has only obscured their vision, not totally severed them from their master. . . . The two disciples love, and the object of their love walks with them; loving, they speak, and the person whom they discuss is there. For Gregory, the stranger is an outward extension of the disciples' inner state" (24). Remember, Luke's story told of how their hearts had burned within their breasts upon hearing the words of Christ. They are unable to "see" Christ, but their hearts recognize him through his words. Gardiner calls this "the pilgrim's response – as by words the heart is enkindled to 'a love it never knew'" (32). He continues:

> Gregory has found in Luke's story an apt example of the pilgrim-life: in their journey Emmaus-ward, the disciples, like the pilgrim human race, have fed upon love-enkindling words; having first seen only a stranger, then their master, they depart, ambivalently nourished yet journeying to future meals and further colloquies. (33)

Of course, real recognition of the living Christ comes at the meal which the three characters share after hospice has been urged upon the stranger. Gardiner talks of a "forceful mandate to hospitality" (25). In the Gregorian pattern the lesson to be learned by normal Christians is evident: "Unlike the historical disciples, his Christian audience does not see the actual Christ; they can see deity only in other stranger-wayfarers, other pilgrims" (25). Finally, in his discussion of the pilgrim plays proper, Gardiner points out that the disciples ". . . have found the *patria*, as always in the tradition, in another man, another traveler [in this case, the risen Christ as Stranger], and through a landscape of love, desire, sight, taste, and words . . ." (140). In the act of finding this *patria*, the pilgrim has had to utilize "right belief and right action" (12) (what I shall call discernment below). Before leaving Gardiner's study it would be worth noting his observation that the word pilgrim means "alien and sojourner" (11), exactly the type of character that will appear time and again in the *LH*.

I shall show below that the *LH* exhibits this "Gregorian pattern of pilgrimage" while at the same time providing its own cluster of key words and concepts: *floresta, desierto, tierra gasta, yermo, pelegrino, romero, palmero, huesped, huespeda, tierra estraña, albergar.* My commentary will show that these terms serve as key structural elements tying the various parts of the *LH* together.

C. Guest/Host Theology

Let us recapitulate. The Emmaus tale is seen as the quintessential pilgrim situation: one encounters a stranger and makes of that person a guest. Let us look at the Latin terms for these concepts. First, **stranger**, as we have seen, is rendered as *peregrinus*. A Latin synonym for this term is *hostis*, which in addition to meaning **stranger**, **foreigner**, and **alien** also came to mean **enemy**. Among the English derivatives of the word are hostile and hostility. The Latin *hospes, hospitis* (and its Romance reflexes: *huesped, huespede, huespeda*, etc.) is a fascinating word; it means at the same time both **guest** and its counterpart, **host**.[7] Its English derivatives include hospitable and hospitality. Again, the quintessential pilgrim situation (and one is to assume the quintessential Christian situation) is to take of this *hostis* and make of that person a *hospes*, that is, take the potential **enemy**, the **stranger,** and make of that person a **guest** (or a **host**), thus bringing that person into a relationship of community in which the normal boundaries of identity are eliminated and the awareness of who owns and who receives goods, for instance, or who dwells and who is visiting in a specific place merge and commingle. Trusting in the abundance provided by God one overcomes mistrust and fear of the **stranger** and the corresponding reaction to hoard and hold tight to one's goods in an effort to keep them safe from the supposed **alien**. In contrast, when one moves in harmony with trust, then not only do **guest** and **host** become one or arrive at-one-ment (atonement), but indeed, there, in that midst can be found the living Christ.

Contemporary theologians Parker J. Palmer and Henri Nouwen discuss the centrality of the guest/host relationship to Christianity and their comments are congruous with the medieval understanding and usage as we shall see in our discussion of the lives of Saints Mary and Martha, the two sisters of Lazarus who were known for providing warm, friendly, intimate hospitality to Jesus. Nouwen describes a situation in which:

---

[7] Despite the fact that both **guest** and **host** are listed as meanings for *huesped* in Spanish dictionaries, contemporary speakers of Spanish are often not aware of this second meaning. There is no problem, however, in the medieval language, where *huesped/huespeda* were typically used for both **guest** and **host**. This is particularly the case in the *LH* where Saint Martha, the hostess, is known as "la buena huespeda" (see fol. 4b and ff) and Christ, her guest, is known as "su buen huesped" (*ibid.*).

> . . . fearful, defensive, aggressive people anxiously cling . . . to
> their property [,] . . . inclined to look at their surrounding world
> with suspicion, always expecting an enemy to suddenly appear,
> intrude and do harm. But still–that is our vocation: to convert
> the *hostis* into a *hospes*, the enemy [or stranger] into a guest and
> to create the free and fearless space where brotherhood and sis-
> terhood can be formed and fully experienced. (46)

He continues:

> When hostility is converted into hospitality then fearful strangers
> can become guests revealing to their hosts the promise they are
> carrying with them. Then, in fact, the distinction between host
> and guest proves to be artificial and evaporates in the recogni-
> tion of the new found unity. (47)

If these references to contemporary theologians seem anachro-
nistic to some, then let us contemplate the words of Justo Pérez de
Urbel, the great historian of Spanish monasticism:

> Al viajero no se le consideraba como un desconocido, sino como
> un hermano. El nombre que se le daba era el de peregrino, indi-
> cador de la fraternidad religiosa que unía al recibido con los que
> le recibían; o bien el de huésped, que daba a entender la confian-
> za, la intimidad y la cordialidad con que se le trataba. Era como
> uno más de la familia monacal: se le daba la misma comida que a
> los monjes y se le admitía en su claustro, en su oratorio y en su
> refectorio. (*El monasterio* 146)

Vázquez de Parga quotes the Rule of St. Benedict concerning hospitality in monasteries as follows: "todos los que [allí] vinieren, sean
recibidos como Jesucristo, pues él mismo dijo: huésped fui y me
recibisteis" (I, 283). One might also take note of the words of St.
Isidore. In his article "La hospitalidad monástica" Antonio Viñayo
González states: "En el libro X de Las Etimologías nos dice que
'*huésped* es el que introduce el pie dentro de la puerta. Y *huésped*
[equivale a hospedero] el que mantiene la puerta patente, de fácil
acceso, abierta, de donde se le da el título de hospitalario'" (40). He
continues:

> El canto a hospitalidad, además de en la *Regla Monástica*, como
> luego veremos, lo incluye san Isidoro al tratar de las obligaciones

del obispo, ya que una de las principales es la hospitalidad: el obispo 'debe dar tales pruebas de hospitalidad que a todo el mundo abra sus puertas con caridad y benignidad. Si todo fiel cristiano debe procurar que Cristo le diga: fui peregrino y me hospedasteis, cuanto más el obispo, cuya residencia es la casa de todos. Un seglar cumple con el deber de hospitalidad abriendo su casa a algún que otro peregrino. El obispo, si no tiene su puerta abierta a todo el que llegue, es un hombre sin corazón.' (*ibid.*)

Gerhart B. Ladner affirms in "*Homo Viator*" that:

every true *peregrinus*, that is to say, the authentic pilgrim and stranger who knocks at the door of the monastery, is to be received as if he was Christ Himself. He must be shown all the respect due to one who may be a wayfarer through this life on the road to the heavenly fatherland. Early mediaeval saints' lives show very clearly that genuine monastic, and generally speaking ascetic, *peregrinatio* was highly esteemed as a radically Christian way of life, which possessed its own *stabilitas*. (242)

It should also be noted here that the traditions associated with medieval pilgrimage insisted on the fact that those who gave hospitality to pilgrims (the hosts and hostesses of strangers) shared in the benefits that accrued to the pilgrim. Sumption affirms that "free hospitality . . . remained throughout the mediaeval period a cornerstone of Christian charity" (198). He quotes the *Pilgrim's Guide* as stating: "Whoever receives them receives St. James and God himself" (*ibid.*).

In this context one must make mention of one of the most famous and most beautiful artistic artifacts of medieval Spain, the romanesque bas-relief sculpture of the Emmaus tale in the cloister of the monastery of Santo Domingo de Silos. The sculpture shows Christ with the two disciples, Cleopas and Luke. Christ's divinity is indicated by means of a cruciform nimbus and his pilgrim status by means of the typical scallop shell emblem on his wallet or traveling bag. (See below, section D, concerning "Traditions of the Road to Santiago" and section F, "The Notion of *Imitatio Christi*.") Holloway describes the sculpture as follows:

In the cloister of Santo Domingo de Silos in Spain a scene is sculpted in stone of the Emmaus Pilgrims' Play acted on Easter

> Mondays in Benedictine Abbeys. It shows Luke carrying the book of his Gospel, Cleophas noting that the sun is setting, and Christ, the unrecognized third, with the cockle shell of the pilgrimage to St. James upon his scrip . . . (19)

One might also recall the Master of Alkmaar's panel of the "Seven Works of Charity" described above.

D. TRADITIONS OF THE ROAD TO SANTIAGO; MORE DETAILS CONCERNING PILGRIMAGE

There are so many traditions associated with the Road to Santiago that it would be impossible to include them all. However, knowledge of some of the essential traditions is necessary in order to familiarize ourselves with the road and those who walked it.

First, there are four traditional routes through France leading to the Pyrenees. The first, the *Via Turonense*, begins at Paris, passes through Tours (from which it takes its name), heads southwest towards Bordeaux, and crosses the Pyrenees at Roncesvalles. The second, the *Via Lemovicense* (taking its name from the Latin form of Limoges), begins in Vézelay (important in the cult of Mary Magdalene) and heads south through the plains of Berry and also crosses the Pyrenees at Roncesvalles. The third traditional route, the *Via Podense*, begins at Le Puy, passes through St. Foy of Conques and Moissac, again crossing the Pyrenees at Roncesvalles. The fourth route, the *Via Tolosana*, begins at Arles, passes through Toulouse (hence its name) and unlike the other three routes, crosses the Pyrenees at Somport. The four routes join in Puente la Reina and form one single road from there on. French pilgrims were so numerous on the various routes that the Road was often called the "Camino francés," the "French Road." An alternate term for the road was the "Via Lactea," "The Milky Way," which takes the east/west configuration of the galaxy as a huge westerly arrow pointing to the saint's tomb in Galicia, at the end of the earth, *finis terrae*. This starry directional sign can therefore also be related to the word Compostela which in an erroneous etymology is thought to derive from *campus stellae* "field of the star."

A pilgrim is distinguished by certain garb which has become traditional: a thick mantel or cloak; a wide-brimmed hat; a staff (*bordón* in Spanish); a gourd, which served as a type of thermos bottle, is often tied to the upper end of the staff; sandals; the traveling pouch, bag, or scrip (Vázquez de Parga 126-129). This garb was as typical of a pilgrim as were the various habits of the religious orders. Indeed, pilgrim status involved initiations and ceremonies that approximate those of holy orders (Sumption 171-172; Holloway 235-38; Vázquez de Parga I 139-143 and III 148) and was protected by special laws (Sumption 171 and *passim*; Starkie 67-68). It was also traditional to represent St. James himself as one of his own devotees, a fellow pilgrim (See below, section F "The principle of *Imitatio Christi*"). For anthropologist Victor Turner (*Process, Performance*) pilgrimage is a liminal or threshold state. Pilgrims pass from a "relatively fixed state of life and social status" to a "condition for which none of the rules and few of the experiences of their previous existence had prepared them" (122). According to him (130), pilgrimage consists of the three phases of a *rite de passage* discovered by A. van Gennep: (1) separation; (2) margin or limen; and (3) reaggregation or reincorporation.

The special emblem of the pilgrim to Santiago was the scallop shell. It was often worn on the brim of the pilgrim's hat or on the cloak. Other times it was tied to the staff. Originally it was the reward a pilgrim received in Santiago for having made a successful pilgrimage, and was carried home as the emblem of that success (Sumption 173-174; Vázquez de Parga I 129-137). Later it came to be an outward sign of pilgrims on way to Santiago.

Pilgrims must have been motivated to take up their journies for various reasons, but two groups can be distinguised according to whether the pilgrim chose freely out of piety to undertake the trip or whether he/she had been commanded to do so as penance for a sin or as exile for a crime. Holloway describes this second type as follows: "There were those who had committed a crime, had been tried in ecclesiastical or secular courts and been sentenced to penitential exile, being thereby as a Cain" (5) (see also Vázquez de Parga I 155-167). Holloway points out that not only Cain, but Adam and Eve, Abraham and Jacob, and the wandering Hebrews looking for the promised land are all "pilgrim figures" (9 and 10). One might add that the Holy Family itself in its flight to Egypt in order to avoid Herod's death sentence against the infant Christ is also a figure of pilgrimage.

The pilgrimage experience carries the individual out of the quotidien and into a new and strange milieu of persons, places, and events in which the pilgrim must create a new and appropriate niche among his/her companions. The experience is that of embryonic community building with all the loyalties, friendships, competitiveness, spite, and so forth that are typical of our daily lives at home, yet somehow magnified and made more intense when walking. Jack Hitt's book, *Off the Road*, is a sustained discussion of the pilgrim experience as community building. He comments:

> A pilgrim is out beyond the fields. He is stripped not merely of the accoutrements but of the assumptions of his society. A pilgrim is cast back upon first principles and then forced to make some sense of the . . . impulse that propelled him down this road. Our little tribe has grown over time, beginning in León. Were we to walk for another year or ten years, I can imagine our rump society metamorphosing into a real one. (235-236)

E. ICONOGRAPHY OF SANTIAGO

The two typical images of Santiago are Santiago Matamoros and Santiago Peregrino. The two images can be classified in part according to the following features:

MATAMOROS (MATAINDIOS)	PEREGRINO
yihad	hajj
warlike	peaceful
monolithic	multicultural
closed militancy (exclusive)	open to other cultures (inclusive)
piedad militante / militancia pía	community of pilgrims
dominance (patriarchal)	shared enterprise (maternal and feminine)
hierarchical	egalitarian
external rejection of other	construction of self in relationship with other
(inability to value alterity; demonization of the other)	(Christ as pilgrim and stranger; theology of the guest/host)

According to William Melczer, Santiago Matamoros "is represented on a galloping horse, usually in profile, entering from left to right, at times in armor, at others with a billowing cape, sword in the right hand and the banner of victory in the left. Behind him the defeated infidels, crushed to the ground, helplessly moan; in front of him the powerless enemy surrenders" (65-66). This image of the saint is "rooted in the . . . Reconquest" (65). In contrast, Santiago Peregrino "is eminently international" and "is characterized by a set of three iconographic attributes . . . : the *bordón*, the *escarcela*, and finally the ever present scallop shell . . ." (66).

In general, if Santiago Matamoros can be seen as the patron of war and of that series of historical events that have come to be called the Reconquest, Santiago Peregrino can be seen on equal footing as the patron of culture who oversaw the influx of Europ-pean, and in particular French styles, tastes, fashions, liturgical practices, literature, art, architecture, music, etc. Matamoros as pa-tron of war and Reconquest can be seen as representing the Chris-tian counterpart to the Muslim *yihad* whereas the pilgrimage to Santiago and its Pilgrim Saint can be seen to mimic the Muslim *hajj*. While Matamoros represents those elements in Spanish culture that responded to the historical situation of the peninsula with a monolithic, closed militancy, Peregrino represents a cultural move-ment that was international in scope, welcoming of foreigners and foreign culture, and relatively inclusive.[8] Matamoros presides over a dominating, patriarchal, hierarchical, pious militancy that rejects and distorts the other,[9] an attitude that will lead Christian

---

[8] This inclusivity could even extend to the culture of the enemy. An example of this would be the *mudejarismo* in such architectural gems as the cathedral of Oloron-Ste. Marie on the French side of the Pyrenees where a victory against the Saracens is celebrated by depicting two of the defeated enemies crouching under the weight of the central column of the portal. In addition to metaphorical support, Saracens provide more substantial support of the building by means of the caliphal vaulting used to span its volume (for illustrations of these two elements see Shaver-Crandell and Gerson, 258). The lobulated (=*mudéjar*) archivolt of the portal of the church of Santiago in Puente la Reina must be mentioned as a second example. One might consider the milieu of Toledo and other cultural centers in the same light. Finally, as Jack Hitt has pointed out in *Off the Road*, the twelfth-century in-scription at the monastery in Roncesvalles envisions and welcomes a truly interna-tional and multicultural multitude by claiming that "Its doors are open to all, well and ill, not only to Catholics, but to pagans, Jews and heretics, the idler and the vagabond and, to put it shortly, the good and the wicked" (24).

[9] I think here of the kind of distortion one can see in a book such as *Historia de la linda Melosina* where Muslims are described as idolators (see Corfis edition, p. 140, col. b). The distortion is particularly astounding when one considers that cen-turies of sharing the Iberian Peninsula with Muslims should have given Christian

Spaniards to expulsion and oppression of minorities, and that will be continued and carried over the ocean-sea to the Americas in later years under the auspices of Santiago Mataindios. [10] Peregrino on the other hand, presides over an egalitarian community of pilgrims who see their trek as a shared enterprise in which individuals construct themselves in relationship with the other. In this nurturing of relationship the Pilgrim Saint is maternal and feminine. It is my belief that these contrasting features of the two iconographic versions of Santiago are representative of what Américo Castro called "the conflictive" aspect of Spanish history:

> The authentic Spaniards . . . molded their own unique shape . . . by opposing simultaneously both Europe and the East, and at the same time letting themselves be affected and seduced by both civilizations. I find that the concept of 'the conflictive' is an increasingly effective way of getting at the core of the maximum creations of the Spaniards. (*Spaniards*, 537)

The "conflictive" aspects between these two iconographic images and their corresponding semiotic systems are similar to the ones that can be perceived between two of the *estados* that made up the medieval social system: *defensores* and *oratores*-the fighters and the prayers. As we shall see below, these two social strata and much

---

Spaniards a more accurate understanding of the realities of Islamic faith and practice. One might reply that the *Melosina* text is a translation from French, which is indeed the case. Nevertheless, from the perspective of the reader, the cultural distortion is successful regardless of its source. Sarah Kay, following Michael Camille, discusses this kind of distortion as follows:

> It is notorious, for example, that the epic Saracen is constructed as a mirror image of the Christian who opposes him. This mirroring effect has been studied by Michael Camille in *The Gothic Idol*: the Saracen 'other' is in effect the 'same' as his Christian opponent, a projection of his fears about himself. Saracens are portrayed as idolaters in apparent contrast to the 'true' religion of the Franks, but the reality of Islam was that it was far more opposed to venerating images than medieval Christianity. The pagan 'trinity' of idols (usually Mahomet, Apollo, and Tervagant) is an uneasy displacement of the Christian division of the godhead into three, and its reliance on religious statuary and icons. (53)

[10] See Diana Fane, ed. *Converging Cultures: Art and Identity in Spanish America*, p. 172 for an illustration of Santiago Mataindios, specifically "St. James the Apostle at Santurwasi" from the Museo Regional of Cuzco, Peru. One need only consult a mildly detailed map of Spanish America to see the number of cities and towns named for Santiago, Matamoros, etc. to affirm the importance of Santiago's patronage of the conquest of America.

of the system of values listed above under the two images will come to have importance in the development of the *LH*.

It is my belief that the compilers consciously took a stand with women, community, egalitarianism, and configured their book in such a way that these values are seen as forming part of the very substance of pilgrimage, one of the defining spiritual expressions of the age.

In addition to the images of St. James himself, the reader must remember that the various roads leading to Santiago would have brought the typical pilgrim into contact with every aspect of medieval art and architecture, from the humblest town church to the very elaborate architectural, artistic, and sculptural programs of the major monasteries and cathedrals. The analyses below will point out several places in the text of the *LH* where the compilers include what amount to verbal renditions of medieval sculpture and painting or at least textual reminders of important themes and motifs that were common in the art of the Road. It is my belief that the average pilgrim with no Latin knew biblical and other holy stories more from texts such as the *LH* and from sculptural programs in monasteries and churches than from any contact with the Bible itself.

F. THE PRINCIPLE OF *IMITATIO CHRISTI*

Both William Melczer in his translation of *The Pilgrim's Guide* and Stephen G. Nichols, Jr. in his book *Romanesque Signs* talk of the notion of *Imitatio Christi*, a concept intimately related to Christocentrism and to Christological ways of thinking. Melczer states:

> Within the pyramidal structure of Christian hierarchical organization, the principles of Christocentrism and sacred Christian history reign supreme. Deriving from them is the notion of *imitatio Christi* which, subsequently, is endlessly reproposed for each of the disciples no less than for the entire host of the faithful: the Lord is followed and imitated by the apostles; the apostles are followed and imitated each by his own disciples; each saint is followed by a throng of his or her own devotees, and so on. (67)

One might ask exactly what part of Christ's life is imitated? The most immediate answer would be to indicate the passion, with its crescendo of suffering, as the part of Christ's life that is reproposed by pilgrimage. But, indeed, the incarnation itself, the coming of God to earth – deity's exile from its true patria – is the most important event imitated when pilgrims leave their homes and countries en route to a distant mecca. Sumption underscores this fact when he states that "only by imitating Christ the man [one should think of Christ as represented at Silos] could one placate Christ the judge [the various Christs-in-majesty on so many a tympanum]. In this way the romantic desire to relive in one's imagination the life of Christ was combined with a real fear of His anger, and a firm conviction that by renouncing one's ordinary life and following His footsteps . . . the force of that anger could be deflected" (135).

Texts of all kinds, geographic locations, specific artistic renditions, can all reflect and teach this notion. Pilgrimage too was part of this process as Sumption points out: "At its highest level, the pilgrim's life . . . was conceived as a continuously repeated drama of the life of Christ" (93). In his discussion of the Clermont-Ferrand *Passion*, Nichols points out that the purpose of the text was ". . . to create a narrative Passion genre capable of illustrating how the . . . rhetoric of the Gospel could be transposed into the present to teach Christians to read in the world the signs of transcendent meaning just as the Gospels had taught" (126). He continues:

> Just as Christ recapitulated sacred and worldly events in himself, so he could teach . . . how those events might be recapitulated in the lives of his imitators. . . . The *Passion* cast Christ as a textualized being, with the consequent implication that texts . . . could be, if not *imitationes Christi* themselves, then certainly, like Christ, the textualized setting in which the lives of "historical" beings could be revealed as recapitulations of christological events in the same way that the Gospels revealed Christ. (*ibid.*)

Roncesvalles, the setting for Roland's famous stand against the Saracens and the most frequently used pilgrim pass over the Pyrenees, also came to take on such significance. Nichols comments:

> It received its meaning from a sacred rewriting: in conjunction with the *Guide*, the site became a textualized itinerary directing the pilgrim's vision and telling him that his progress through this place was a symbolic one; a projection of himself back onto the sacred time of *in illo tempore*, when real heroes and martyrs, his

Christian predecessors, waged a literal battle against nature and nonbelievers to win the prize of eternal life and the heavenly crown. (155)

In the analysis of the *LH* below I shall show how the notion of *imitatio Christi* was a central concern of the compilers in their effort to instruct pilgrims concerning the real meaning and importance of their endeavor. The stories recapitulate the biblical events and do so chronologically. The first tales in the book are about individuals who were companions of Christ and who witnessed and took part in the biblical events themselves (the tales of Mary and Martha). Next there are tales concerning individuals who lived later in time and further west in the Mediterranean world: Mary the Egyptian and Catherine of Alexandria. As we shall see, their travails and experiences are cast as *imitationes Christi*. The next two tales, the story of St. Eustace and the romance of King William of England (tales that are closely related to one another), move the chronology first to the Roman world and then to the medieval mythic world of England. At the same time the setting of the tales has moved even further west in Europe. Again, we shall see that their travails are seen as paralleling the lives of Christ and the saints. The next tales are romances that take place in what was conceived of as late classical Rome (*Otas* and the *Santa enperatris*) and finally, the culminating text (the *Carlos Maynes*) takes place in what for medieval readers was almost their own time in a "real" place – the France of Charlemagne. Again, the analysis below will show that these texts also continue the process of *imitatio Christi*. The next step, and one I believe was experienced by medieval readers, was to contemplate their own situation and endeavors as falling in line with this trajectory – a carrying forward of the holy life paralleling the way in which the *translatio studii* carried forward the intellectual traditions of antiquity. In this way, the readers and hearers of the *LH* are able to project their own travails back into time (Nichols' *in illo tempore*) while the stories of the saints and other pious heroines and heroes are projected forward onto them – a two way street, if you will, although I believe a circle is a better image for what is the real structural framework of the *LH*, as we shall see in the analysis of the book's final chapter, the story of Carlos Maynes and his wife Seuilla and their son Loys (see below, chapter IV.H).

Sumption affirms the fact that it is quite traditional to view pilgrimage as an *imitatio Christi*: "They often referred to their pilgrimage as an *imitatio Christi*. By re-enacting in their own lives the suffering of Christ they felt that they were performing an act of personal redemption" (92-93). He goes on to say that "the journey of the ideal pilgrim could be presented . . . as an elaborate allegory of the life of Christ from the Nativity to the Resurrection" (*ibid.*).

As mentioned above, the *LH* presents sections of text that are verbal renditions of medieval sculpture. The purpose of those segments of text is in line with the processes of theosis (see below, section G) and *imitatio Christi*. These "verbal sculptures" work in tandem with the plots of the various tales by both reaching back as recapitulations of the life of Christ, and at the same time carrying forward all the way to the pilgrim reader/hearer. That is to say, the *LH* sets up a complex grid of stories interspersed with reminders of sculpture and other plastic images pilgrims might have seen on their itinerary – a grid of textual and visual correspondences–with which it hopes to teach and encourage its pilgrim community. The analyses below will indicate several segments of the text that make use of these complex correspondences. If this correspondence of the visual and the verbal seems far-fetched to some, let them consider Sumption's assurance that the idea of medieval people seeing themselves in terms of the life of Christ "conceals one of the profoundest sentiments of an age which *reduced all spiritual ideas to images*" (94) [my emphasis]. One might also consider the arguments of Michael Camille in "Seeing and Reading" in which he addresses "whether equivalences existed between different forms of visual art and the varying reading skills of their audiences" (26). His conclusion is that such equivalences do indeed exist and that both are "secondary representations . . . referring back to the spontaneous springs of speech" (32). Taking his lead from Susan Noakes, he stresses the communal and collective appreciation of both texts and images (32-33) in which the quasi-literate or illiterate are dependent upon the reading, interpretation, and explications provided by others (33). Camille suggests that the purpose of the "constantly repeated schemata used by the Romanesque artist served a similar purpose to the oral mnemonic formulae in literary composition" (34-35), namely the cultivation or nurturing of the visual and oral memories of the viewers and reader/hearers (34). These schemata or formulae are the equivalents to the recurring images, plot patterns, situations, keywords, etc. that are woven throughout the *LH*.

As an example of these schemata (other than similar patterns of plot and imagery) I would point out the oft repeated list of biblical examples cited by the characters of the various tales of the *LH* whenever they are threatened with persecution, torture, or worse. Inevitably they cite the prophet Daniel in his famous den of lions and the "tres njños de baujloña," Shadrach, Meshak, and Abednego. These references are so numerous that any reader will quickly come to know the references and their referents. For Daniel, see folios 20v; 81v; 93v; 106r; 112r and for the "tres njños" see 21v; 31r; 93v; 112v. The readers would also be reminded of the martyrdom of St. Eustace and his family in a brass oven reminiscent of the situation of the "tres njños" (see below, chapter IV.D).

In another article ("Philological Iconoclasm") Camille discusses the practice of excising medieval texts from their objective context in manuscripts [and, we might add, in oral delivery], a practice that has its origin in editorial practices of the late nineteenth century. He points out how a text that might be illustrated with illuminations and miniatures or "richly colored" and characterized by "variable graphic movements" could be reduced to a regularized edition of "the purely optical . . . that marks the modern printed book as alien to the medieval mode of rapturous reading, rooted as it was in a somatic and sensuous experience" (382). He describes such editions using morbid terminology such as "embalmed," "epitaphs," and "grave" (*ibid.*). Earlier he talks of "how modern philology has erased all aspects of enactment – sound, sight, and sense – from this medieval text [The *Vie de Saint Alexis* or the *St. Albans Psalter*]" (375). My inclusion of these complex correspondences of the verbal and the visual is an attempt (1) to recapture some of this sensuousness in reading; (2) to imagine some aspects of the enactment of the *LH*; and (3) to give renewed life to a text that has too long been buried in the sepulcher of multiple and disparate editions in the tradition of the "image/text split" (Camille 385).

G. EGALITARIANISM

There is a problem with the notion of *imitatio Christi*, especially as concerns the Road to Santiago and the iconography of St. James.

In the hierarchical world of medieval Christendom it is peculiar to depict a saint of the stature of St. James as one of many other pilgrims. It is worth recalling that St. James was not just one of the many saints, but one of the three "preferred" apostles of Christ by virtue of having been chosen to witness the Transfiguration (the other two are Peter and John, James' brother). Melczer discusses this matter as "an inherent theological problem" (67), suggesting that it must be ascribed to "extraordinary mass devotion" (*ibid.*). He then dicusses the even more "clamorous aberration of the Christocentric principles that govern Christian sacred history . . . ," namely the depiction of Christ himself ". . . not merely as a wayfarer, . . . [but] . . . as a devotee of one of His three preferred disciples" (68). Melczer's reference, of course, is to the famous Emmaus relief at Santo Domingo de Silos which depicts Christ not only with the staff and wallet of a pilgrim in general, but with the scallop shell emblem which signals him as a pilgrim to Santiago specifically. However, I believe medieval people did not see the "theological aberration" (68) that bothers Melczer. Instead they were guided by the principles of guest/host theology and commensality to appreciate an element inherent in *imitatio Christi* that eludes him, namely the "radical egalitarianism" of the Christian tradition (see Crossan, *Historical Jesus*, 345-348 and *Jesus*, 71-74). Pilgrims are followers of James who is a follower of Christ. When Christ is depicted as a pilgrim, he is shown as one of his own devotees, thus indicating to all pilgrims their own likeness to him. Fray Justo Pérez de Urbel has described the Silos Emaus relief as follows:

> En el texto evangélico la palabra peregrino significaba extranjero; pero el escultor, que entendía de arte más que de filología, nos representó al Señor como uno de aquellos peregrinos que, después de haber visitado el cuerpo del Apóstol Santiago, daban un rodeo y se llegaban hasta Silos para postrarse ante las cenizas del Taumaturgo castellano, que estaban calientes todavía. Y debía de ser para ellos *una gran alegría verse retratados en aquella doble imagen*, que representaba a su Salvador. (*El claustro* 97) [my emphasis]

The analysis of the various texts below will elucidate in which ways the *LH* presents this egalitarianism and how I see it forming part of that confluence of cultural and artistic phenomena that make up romanesque-form culture.

In the early pages of *Romanesque Signs*, Nichols discusses the concept of theosis, a term he defines as a ". . . mystical conjunction of the ascending individual with the descending godhead . . ." (11). He quotes John Scottus Eriugena: "The Word descended into man in order that, through it, man could raise himself to God" (10). He goes on to say that "for the early part of the eleventh century . . . the narrative possibilities of theosis were confined to the beings of king and saint" (11). This, of course, is consistent with what we know of the hierarchical social arrangements of the Middle Ages. André Vauchez confirms this class bias in "Lay People's Sanctity": "While by no means all noblemen were considered saints by the church, it had become almost impossible for someone not of noble stock to acquire a certain repute in this domain, so firmly entrenched became the conviction that moral and spiritual perfection could flourish only in one of noble birth and illustrious descent" (26). However, he claims that the situation changed in the Mediterranean countries:

> In the Mediterranean regions during the twelfth century, there appeared and developed the practice of venerating commoners, especially members of the middle class and craftsmen. A whole hagiography, which up to now has remained little known and has received little attention, developed in these countries devoted to figures like Saint Dominic de la Calzada . . . . (27)

He continues:

> As the lives dedicated to them reveal, these eminent people shared certain characteristics. All had been either pilgrims or ascetics. Most important, they had devoted themselves to the service of their neighbors, whether by building bridges, roads, and hospices to facilitate the journeys of travelers and pilgrims, or by attacking the problems caused by the chaotic development of towns and helping the misfits and victims of the economic boom that was widening even further the gap between the social classes. As their enthusiastic practice of charitable works showed, behind all these initiatives lay the conviction that the poor were images of Christ and a privileged means of access to God. (28)[11]

---

[11] Note how this description by Vauchez is matched by the following decription by Wifredo Rincón García in his "Aproximación a la iconografía de dos santos":

In the *LH* I believe the compilers were intent on showing that through the principle of *imitatio Christi* all pilgrims, regardless of social background, could take part in this "mystical conjunction" by following Christ (their fellow pilgrim), the saints, and the heroic queens, kings, and commoners depicted in the various chapters of the text. We shall outline this project of egalitarianism in the analyses below, making specific reference to the doctrine of *natura*, to episodes in which *legos* are compared favorably to *clerigos*, and by paying particular attention to the dynamic between *nobles* and *villanos*.

H. Misogyny and Feminism

It is not to my interest nor part of my plan to outline the history and presence of misogyny and antifeminism in the Spanish Middle Ages. The reader interested in this topic is referred to the studies of Bloch, Goldberg, Ornstein, Muriel Tapia, and Lacarra listed in the Bibliography. The *LH,* taking a strong stand in opposition to misogyny, can be placed in the list of pro-feminist works provided by Ornstein (220-221). The *LH* criticizes the tradition of courtly love, but unlike so many works of the fifteenth century, it aims its critique almost entirely at males, showing that what Gerli (1987) calls

---

Los peregrinos, en su camino hacia Santiago, rumbo a lo que para ellos era desconocido, recorrían países distintos, con diferentes idiomas y costumbres, enfrentándose a las inclemencias del tiempo, al peligro en los caminos accidentados, ríos que cruzar y montes y desfiladeros que necesariamente había que salvar. Expuestos a las enfermedades y al cansancio que, podía llegar hasta el agotamiento, a la lluvia, la nieve, el sol, los bandidos y también a los posaderos que sin escrúpulos, en muchas ocasiones, abusaban de los pobres peregrinos a los que podían llegar a matar – quedando el asesinato impune – para apoderarse de sus pertenencias.

Así, a lo largo de los siglos fueron muchos los anónimos sacerdotes y religiosos que cuidaron de los peregrinos en la ruta jacobea, quedando tan solo de ellos un indefinido recuerdo. Sin embargo, dos importantes hombres dejaron una indeleble huella para la historia de las peregrinaciones a Santiago, distinguiéndose por sus atenciones a los viajeros y por el esfuerzo que llevaron a cabo para mejorar las incómodas condiciones de los lugares que debían atravesar. (222)

The two are Santo Domingo de la Calzada and San Juan de Ortega, the disciple of Santo Domingo. Worthy of note is how closely the travails of pilgrims described here match the travails of so many of the characters portrayed in the *LH*.

a "protesta social y religiosa que defiende la concepción cristiana del amor" (47) need not be misogynist in nature. [12] Without doubt, one of the intentions of the compilers of the text was to take a strong stand in favor of women since the pilgrim people is made up of both males and females. The analyses below will present some very useful episodes that seem to use the arguments favored by the misogynists against males themselves.

I. FAMILY SEPARATION, WANDERING, TRAVAILS

As we have seen above, the word pilgrim, (*peregrinum* in Latin or *peregrino* in Spanish) meant among other acceptations "exile." Many of the stories presented in the *LH* are of family separation in which the various members of a family wander from place to place and from one to another situation in which they are given hospice by a variety of characters. The wandering causes great hardship and stress and is one of the many travails which are meted out to the protagonists of the tales. In almost all cases these situations are seen to parallel the situation of the pilgrim and the analyses below will show in what ways this takes place.

---

[12] See also Gerli, "'Religión del amor'".

CHAPTER IV

ANALYSIS OF *EL LIBRO DE LOS HUESPEDES*

A. THE STORIES OF MARY AND MARTHA–BUILDING A TEXTUAL COMMUNITY

As noted above, perhaps the most obvious guest/host relationship in the Bible is the story of the sisters of Lazarus, Mary and Martha, and their hosting of Jesus. Note that the initial texts in the *LH* deal with the tales of Saints Mary and Martha, [1] thus providing an appropriate invitation into the text to the reader/pilgrim. It should be noted that the codex has a lacuna of four folios that eliminates the latter portion of the life of Saint Mary and the first part of the life of Saint Martha. The missing folios have been restored in the editions of Walsh/Thompson (another Spanish version) and Rees Smith (an Old French version).

The *LH* commences with a presentation of the Life of Saint Mary Magdalene beginning with her arrival in southern France accompanied by a group of disciples in an effort to evangelize there. At first they are denied hospitality, but eventually come to have success in their evangelization, even convincing the lord of Marseille to go off on a pilgrimage to consult with St. Peter. His character is identified as a *romero*. His trip is marked by family separation and hardship, travails in which St. Mary comforts him: ". . . ella confortaua el Romero que non dexase lo que començara . . ." [fol. 2c]. It is at this point that the lacuna interrupts the narrative in the *LH*, but in the W/T reconstruction we learn that the wife of the lord is left

---

[1] Mary Magdalene here is an amalgam of various biblical Marys. See Walsh/Thompson, 1-3 for more details on this composite saint.

as if dead even though her soul miraculously accompanies her husband on his pilgrimage.

In the tale of St. Martha we find out that Christ was the guest of Mary and Martha and we are told that it is in their house that he establishes "religion":

> . . . asi dexo las casas delos rreys & delos otros prinçepes do podiera posar & quiso posar & comer & beuer & folgar en casa de santa marta & alli estableçio el toda rreligion & abrio los sacramentos de santa eglesia & en aquella casa fizo el vna eglesia de dos maneras de vida que llaman en latin contenplatiua & activa . . . [fol. 3a]

Michel, admitting that there is a lack of clarity in the text, conjectures that although ". . . the meaning of this sentence is not clear" nevertheless, ". . . the word *religion* has to do with the manner of life from the spiritual stand-point, and the reference may be to an interpretation of Luke 10: 41 f" (74).

My suggestion would be that the text means as it reads: in the context of a commingled guest/host community Christ established "toda rreligion" and "abrio los sacramentos de santa eglesia." The roles of Martha (and to a lesser extent her sister Mary) as hostess and that of Christ as guest are stressed through the constant use of terms such as "huespeda de ihesu xpisto" [fol. 3b]; "su bendita huespeda" [fol. 3d]; "la buena huespeda" [fol. 4b]; etc. for Martha and "su bendito huesped" [fol. 3a]; "su buen huesped(e)" [fol. 3d, 5a]; etc. for Christ.

The text continues with some detail as to what this "rreligion" might be by pointing out that "en estas dos vidas [those of Mary and Martha] son todas las reglas de rreligion & de orden & los enseñamjentos del viejo testamento & del nueuo . . . sy nos amaremos nuestro proximo asi como a nos mesmo & ayudarmos segunt nuestro poder" [fol. 3b]. It suggests that the guest/host relationship is the embodiment of the Golden Rule, exemplified in Martha and Mary as representative of the active life (Martha's detailed domestic preparedness) and the contemplative life (Mary's devotion to Christ's presence) respectively. Underscored is the fact that Martha's hospitality was not limited to Christ: ". . . ella auia alli grant hospedado asi como en Bretaña.[2] Su mesa era comunal a todos . . ." [fol. 4d]. The tale concludes by stating:

---

[2] See Morrás (120) for a discussion of this "error."

> Ora sabed todos que aqui es la vida de santa marta la bendita
> huespeda de ihesu xpisto / que nos mostro las buenas fazañas
> dela vida actiua / ca bien pareçio por ella / & por sus obras / que
> los que Resçebieren su castigo / que resçibiran los pobres en sus
> posadas asy como deuen / syn dubdar ninguna cosa & yran al
> Regno delos çielos alli o dios les dira / venjd adelante benditos
> amigos de mj padre & tomad el Regno delos çielos que uos tien
> aparejado / Quando yo oue fanbre uos me distes a comer . . .
> [fol. 7b]

This suggests that the act of receiving the poor in one's home is a
manner of taking possession here and now of the Kingdom of God
("venjd adelante . . . & tomad el Regno . . ."). In other words, this
first text in the *Pilgrims' Companion* (I consider the two lives to be
a unified chapter) establishes a Guest/Host Theology which sees
the construction of the Kingdom in this world as contingent upon
providing hospice to the poor and unrecognized, thus repeating in
another key part of what Gardiner has called "the Gregorian pattern of pilgrimage," finding the "patria" (or "Regno") in other persons and other travelers–in this case, the poor of Jesus Christ.[3]

Among the other aspects of this section dedicated to Mary and
Martha, we are told that Martha gave up her wealth in the Holy
Land in order to evangelize in "tierras estrañas" [fol. 3d]. In following this calling she is "apostolessa con los apostolos & diçipula con
los deçipulos" [fols. 3b-3c] and her actions parallel those of Adam
("el primer ome"), the children of Israel as they wandered in search
of the promised land (the "tierra deleytosa"), and the Lord himself
(see fol. 3d). We are also told that in addition to great beauty,
among her many attributes Martha "auja aguda la lengua & era sse-
suda en fablar" [fol. 4a]. In other words, the text makes plain that
Martha is a female Apostle at the same time that it underscores her
great intelligence and persuasive abilities. It also makes clear the
ways in which her evangelization in foreign lands is a recapitulation
of so many of the key Biblical stories, many of which are seen also
as pilgrimage stories.

---

[3] I think it quite possible that the *LH* could be construed to provide historical
roots for one of the Hispanic world's major contributions to theological thought in
the twentieth century, namely Liberation Theology. Gustavo Gutiérrez has traced
this line of theology at least as far back as Bartolomé de las Casas in his *Las Casas:
In Search of the Poor of Jesus Christ.* A liberationist interpretation of the *LH* would
push back the time line of liberation-type theological thinking an additional 200-
250 years.

Thus we see that the stories of Mary and Martha, the initial episodes of the *LH*, present characters who are pilgrims, underscore the guest/host relationship between the sisters and their holy guest, and develop a theology that sees the guest/host relationship as fundamental to the development of Christian practice. In fact, these tales convey the idea that such a relationship is almost a type of super-sacrament. It is worth noting that the contexts of all four of the Biblical texts listed as relevant to pilgrimage are matched in these initial folios. In addition, the text takes a pro-feminine stand in declaring Martha an "apostolessa" and a "diçipula" while underscoring her evangelization as a type of pilgrimage and as an imitation or recapitulation of Biblical history and the life of Christ. If, as I contend, the *LH* was intended and received as a series of readings for the evening entertainment and edification of pilgrims, one would have to agree that these early folios (perhaps the first two evenings' readings) appeal directly to the pilgrims in terms of their self-esteem (since they see reflections of themselves in the texts) and in terms of what they hoped would be their experience as strangers and guests on the Road to Santiago. In this way the text goes about building a positive and optimistic spirit of community among the pilgrims whom we must assume to be from various geographic locations and social strata of medieval Spain. We shall see exactly what other features might characterize this community in our analysis of subsequent texts. However, the explicit mention of the poor in this passage looks ahead to the importance egalitarianism will assume in the ideology developed in the *LH*, and reflects yet again the contrast between the hierarchical, warrior Matamoros and the egalitarian, peace making Peregrino. If these suggestions seem extreme, note that Sumption mentions the fact that collections of saints' lives had "the effect of greatly simplifying doctrinal issues and often unintentionally encouraged *heterodox* notions" (44) [my emphasis].

B. Santa Maria Egiçiaca: Pilgrims, Art, and Equality

The *Estoria de Santa Maria Egiçiaca* may be the best known of the hagiographic stories in the *LH*. It tells the story of an extremely beautiful young woman who joyfully throws herself into a life of lascivious, sinful behavior only to come to a conversion experience and thereafter dedicate herself to a life of hardships and loneliness as penance for her earlier laxity. In this latter stage of her life what had been her extreme beauty turns into repulsive ugliness. In addition to the prose text of the *LH*, the tale is represented in medieval Spanish in a verse version and in another variant prose version (see Snow "Notes" for a description of these various traditions and below, chapter VII "A review of modern editions").

For the purposes of this study we shall highlight several aspects of the text which bear upon our themes. First, the text privileges the presence of pilgrims and pilgrimage as the persons and the event that draw Mary towards her conversion experience. The young Mary has spurned her parents' plea that she turn from her life of sin and instead abandons both home and family in order to pursue her life of pleasure in Alexandria. There she encounters a retinue of pilgrims in the port and she offers her body to all of them if they are willing to take her along with them to Jerusalem: ". . . yo so fermosa mançeba & menjna meu cuerpo les abaldonare / que no he al que les dar" [fol. 8c]. Indeed, the voyage to Jerusalem is marked by quite graphic cupidity: ". . . non ouo y viejo njn mançebo que aquella noche non pecase con ella . . ." [fol. 8d].

Upon arrival in the Holy Land, Mary continues her life as a prostitute where, we are told: ". . . toda la mançebia de la tierra era ençendida por su beldat . . ." [fol. 9a]. On Ascension Day she attempts to worship along with the throng of faithful, but she is not allowed into the temple: ". . . semejauale que veya caualleros que tenjan espadas desnudas en las manos & quele vedauan la entrada . . ." [fol. 9a]. This sets off a chain reaction of thoughts which lead the lascivious girl to a penitent attitude although doubts continue as to whether salvation can come to such a one as she. At this point she catches sight of an image of the Holy Mother to whom she addresses a long, soulful, doctrinally accurate confession which indicates her resolve to abandon her life of sin and be a new person. She requests the mediation of the "mother and daughter" of the Lord, at which point she is able to enter the church and worship. As she leaves the church she passes the image of the Virgin and requests instruction as to what to do and where to go. The voice of the Virgin miraculously addresses her at that point, instructing her to take communion and then to take up residence in the desert as penance for her sins: ". . . y andaras en quanto bjujeres & alynpiar te as de todos tus pecados . . ." [fol. 9d]. An anonymous pilgrim (*pelegrino*) then steps forward to give her three coins with which she buys three loaves of bread that sustain her during the first year of her wandering in the desert (variously called *desierto, yermo,* and *floresta*).

The text highlights the fact that whenever Mary's resolve weakens she remembers the image of the Virgin in whose presence her conversion took place: ". . . nunca se le olujdo santa maria Ante se le menbraua de la Jmagen que ella metiera en fiaduria./ & todos los dias del mundo Rogaua a santa maria que oujese della merçet & piadat" [fol. 10b]. This reference to an image of the Virgin is accompanied in other portions of the text by descriptions that are reminiscent of yet other aspects of medieval art. Upon reading the following description can any pilgrim to Santiago not think of one of the many Pantocrator Christs depicted in countless tympanums? "& llorauan muy duramente quando les menbraua del dia del juyzio / do todos los angeles tremerian de pauor quando verna el fijo de dios en su majestad & veran el fuego perdurable / do los malos seran tormentados perdurable mente" [fol. lla].

Let us recapitulate. Up to this point we have a text that presents a conversion that happens as a result of pilgrimage (however cynically undertaken), a miracle, and the contemplation of a holy image. The person converted must do penance by wandering in a *floresta* or *desierto* where she experiences great hardship and travails, is aided by a pilgrim, and is comforted in her travails by holding in her mind's eye the earlier artistic image. I would contend that any pilgrim reader/hearer would comprehend this text in terms of his/her experience of the pilgrimage road and would do so not only through the verbal text itself, but also through the rich references the text makes to artistic monuments of the kind so plentiful on the pilgrim way. This is exactly the kind of "complex correspondences" I mentioned above in chapter III.F the purpose of which is not only that of instruction and entertainment but also that of the affirmation of pilgrims in their principle endeavor – community building.

To return to the tale of the Egyptian, Mary comes to know a certain Zozimas who lives in a monastery at the edge of the *floresta*. Upon their first meeting they have a disagreement as to which one should be the first to bless the other. Mary believes it should be Zozimas since, obviously, he is a priest: ". . . non era Razon que yo primera mente benediçion te de / ca tu eres clerigo de misa . . ."

[fol. lld]. Zozimas, on the other hand, wants the blessing of this hermit saint since he perceives her special holiness. Mary resolves the conflict by calling upon God to bless them both. Walker (*Egiçiaca* li-lii) has pointed out that the text of the *LH* abbreviates here the more detailed description of a priest's functions that can be appreciated in the poetic *Vida*. He speculates that the reason for this abbreviation has to do with the intended audience of the text. He believed the *LH* was ". . . intended either for private devotional reading or for reading aloud to a small group of attentive educated listeners, such as one might find in a monastery or a palace, a very different kind of performance from the minstrel's recitation to a mass illiterate audience in the market place" (lv). I quote at length here since this argument is a reiteration of some of the claims he made in an earlier article dealing with the contrast between oral delivery of medieval literature and private reading (Walker "Oral Delivery"). There, too, he insisted on the "educated" status of the groups read to. In his edition of the *Egiçiaca* he defines these groups as ". . . a more cultivated public, less in need of instruction in basic theology, capable of following more sophisticated syntactic patterns . . . and sufficiently 'captive' not to require highly-coloured concrete details to maintain their interest" (liv-lv).

My reading of this particular passage of the *LH* is quite different, as is my understanding of its intended audience and their educational level. [4] First, Mary, a wandering penitent in a "tierra estraña," is symbolically a pilgrim. Through her travails she has won for herself a certain holiness that is easily perceived by onlookers (Zozimas). This holiness gives her a status that is not dependent on her class origins, the whole point of the interchange between the two characters. It is the first instance of an argument that will be

---

[4] Walker returns to this theme in his discussion of the *Otas* text in "From French Verse. . . ." See below, chapter V, "The matter of translation" for my comments concerning his analysis. Comparing Escorial MSS h.I.13 and K.II.12 might help illuminate the issue of private reading v. public reading or performance. MS h.I.13 is a large format codex similar to the breviaries commonly seen in cathedral and monastic museums while K.II.12 is quite small in comparison, more appropriate for both a private collection, and, perhaps, private reading. The larger format of h.I.13 was probably meant for a public reading similar to the reading done in monastic refectories. Also, h.I.13 is a "budget" codex, lacking illumination. In fact, the codex remains unfinished in terms of rubrication and initials. One would expect a book aimed at a private collection to be more of a luxury item.

taken up later in the *LH*, namely the absence of any difference between clerics and laypersons, particularly in terms of learnedness,
one aspect of the *LH*'s case for egalitarianism:

> . . . dios nunca fizo cosa sin rrazon / esto deue saber qual quier
> lego Mas de saber los fechos de dios njn ssus poridades poco
> mas sabe y el clerigo que el lego / si muy letrado non es / Ca el
> poder de dios & ssus poridades / & los ssus juyzios sson escuros
> tanto & tan encobiertos que bien puedo dezir / que tanto ssabe
> ende el lego como el clerigo . . . [fol. 113d]

One might assume that this argument would resonate in the
hearts of all pilgrim readers and hearers who have spent a mem-
orable portion of their lives walking past and being hospiced in all
manner of shrines, monasteries, cathedrals, churches, etc. where
they contemplated the remains of saints, gazed upon the sculptural
programs (none other than illustrated Bibles), and both heard and
read (or had read for them) the stories of the saints and other pious
heroes of their culture. What individuals, having undertaken a successful pilgrimage to Santiago (or to Rome or Jerusalem), would be
willing to cede easily to their local parish priests in questions of the
spirit? Sumption affirms our conclusion when he states: "A surprisingly large number of pilgrims seem to have left their homes solely
in order to deny their parish priest his monopoly over their spiritual
welfare" (13).

I might also point out that it is in a later portion of the *LH*, usually called *De vna santa enperatris*, that we have the most explicit
definition of what a pilgrim is. I present it at this point for I fear
that many readers might recoil at the easy way in which I have "assumed" Mary the Egyptian to be a symbolic pilgrim. The text talks
about the husband of the santa enperatris, the emperor of Rome
who has decided to make a trip to the Holy Land. It reads as follows:

> Ca aueno asi como plugo a dios / que entro al enperador en vo-
> luntad de yr en rromeria a Jerusalen / & de visitar los santos & las
> santas por que fuese su alma heredera enel Regno delos çielos /
> E quiso trabajar su cuerpo andando por muchas tierras estrañas
> que el alma ende ouiese gualardon / E el enperador se guyso
> muy bien por yr demandar su criador / E leuo consigo / grant

conpaña & muy buena / & mucho oro / & mucha plata. [fol. 100c][5]

Note that a pilgrim is a person intent on bringing trials and travails upon his/her body by wandering in (or through) strange places (tierras estrañas) with good companions, visiting the shrines of the saints, and in so doing becoming an inheritor of the Kingdom (Regno). I might point out, as does Benaim de Lasry in her edition of the *Santa enperatris* (51 and 58-59), that the source text of this passage (Gautier de Coinci's *De l'Anpereriz de Rome*) does not use the word **rromeria** (pilgrimage):

> Car il avint, si com Dieu plot,
> Que volenté l'Emperere ot
> De sainz et saintes visiter
> Par s'ame el ciel fere hériter,
> Travaillier volt lou cors en terre
> En visiter et en requerre
> Par divers liex, par païs mainz
> Et loinz et près saintes et sainz.
>
> (ll. 117-124)

The *LH*, a text that privileges pilgrims as characters and as audience, invokes a more precise term than its source text for what amounts to a definition of one of the more characteristic expressions of medieval religious life.

Perhaps it is easier now to understand why Mary the Egyptian can be perceived as an exemplary pilgrim, at least symbolically. It might also be possible to understand at this point why it is imperative to read the *LH* as an integrated text. If in our reading of the texts which heretofore have been considered independent tales we limit ourselves to comments on source texts, translation techniques, competing versions of the individual tales, etc. then we fail to per-

---

[5] Note how closely this description of pilgrimage matches that of Alfonso el Sabio en the Siete Partidas as quoted by Vázquez de Parga:

> Romeros e Pelegrinos son omes que fazen sus romerias e pelegrinajes, por seruir a Dios e honrrar los Santos, e por sabor de fazer esto, estrañanse de sus logares, e de sus mugeres, e de sus casas, e de todo lo que han, e uan por tierras ajenas, lazerando los cuerpos, o despendiendo los aueres, buscando los Santos. . . . (I, 119)

ceive the book's unity and we fail to comprehend the innovative and important contributions it makes to the history and traditions of the pilgrimage to Santiago, to the literary history of Spain, and to our understanding of translation and the place it occupies in the vernacular cultural production of the Middle Ages.[6] Likewise, we might also fail to comprehend the book's various themes and its intended audience.

To return to the tale of the Egyptian, Mary has made the acquaintance of Zozimas, as we have seen above. She instructs him as to various other meetings by miraculously foretelling future events, and then maintains her solitude for long periods of time. At their second meeting, Zozimas has come to the *floresta* in order to give Mary communion. He is quite concerned when he cannot find her. However, she does arrive, and as John R. Maier has stated: "Finally Mary appears on the other side of the river, and miraculously crosses it without wetting her feet. The analogy with Christ's walk on the Sea of Galilee is obvious" ("Sainthood, Heroism" 430). This is a case of *imitatio Christi* as the text makes clear through the words of Zozimas: "& dixo verdadera mente non mentio dios que prometio que aquellos lo semejarian que se espulgauan de sus pecados . . ." (fol. 13r).

At the end of Mary's life it is Zozimas' charge to find her body and bury it and then to spread the news of her holy penance. At first he is unable to find her and so laments with the words: "Buen señor dios padre muestra me el thesoro ascondido que me ante mostraste & muestra me el cuerpo que todo el mundo non poderia conprar/" [fol. 13c]. As Maier has pointed out, "Mary is described in terms of the traditional goals of heroes. She is a treasure, some boon that the hero will bring back with him by which society will benefit" ("Sainthood, Heroism" 431). In addition to the psychological conclusions drawn by Maier, the word *thesoro* as applied to Mary's body probably reminded the pilgrim audience of the ornate coffers and chests that served as the reliquaries for the mortal remains of the saints all along the pilgrim route. This is another example of the complex correspondences between the textual and the visual that are utilized by the compilers of the *LH*. In addition, this use of the lexical item *thesoro* anticipates a more symbolic use of the term in a later portion of the *LH* (see chapter IV.H, p. 102 below).

---

[6] See below, chapter V, "The Matter of Translation."

Zozimas does find Mary's body, and laments not having a means by which to dig a grave: ". . . mas que fare laso mesquino que non tengo casa con que faga la cueua en quanto el asi dezia contra sy vio yazer vn baston pequeño en tierra / & fuesse luego tomarlo / . & començo de cauar conel . . ." [fols. 13d-14a]. Indeed, even with the *baston* he is unable to dig a grave in the hard, dry earth until a lion magically appears and digs a grave with its claws, and the holy body is buried. Zozimas thereupon returns to his monastery to spread the news of Mary the Egyptian: "& zozimas el buen ome se torno para su monesterio / bendiziendo mucho nuestro señor. / cantando hymnos & loando nuestro señor ihesu xpisto % & tanto que llego al abadia conto al abad / & a los fraires todo quanto viera & oyera . . . " [fol. 14b]. It is worthy of note that a *baston*, the typical accoutrement of a pilgrim, comes to him at this point and that after the burial he returns to his monastery as a type of singing pilgrim filled with astounding news of spiritual truth. As with the word *thesoro*, both the *baston* and the act of singing are aspects of this character that foreshadow future, more complex characters in later sections of the book (see chapter IV.H below).

The last commentary to be made concerning this section on Mary the Egyptian has to do with the transformation of Mary from the lithesome, lascivious beauty to the repugnantly ugly saint:

> . . . & su carne que era blanca como nieue finco toda negra caruon por la friura del jnbierno & por la calentura del verano ssus cabellos / tornaron blancos ssu rostro torno anpollado & su boca quebrada / & sus ojos fueron couados / & su pecho prieto & aspro que semejaua cuero de caçon / & los braços & las manos & los dedos auja mas secos que podia ser / & las vñas auja luengas / & el vientre traya caydo & sus pies eran Resquebrados & muchas llagas por ellos . . . [fol. 10b]

Here in the early folios of the book ugliness is established as a possible sign of holiness.[7] In chapter IV.H below we shall again take up the issue of ugliness and its connection to holiness and decency and the correlate issue of discernment which will be necessary in order to distinguish true signs from those meant to deceive and lead astray.

---

[7] See Robertson for other corporeal aspects of female saints.

C. DE SANTA CATALJNA, LEARNING AND *IMITATIO CHRISTI*: MAKING THE CASE FOR WOMEN

The next section of the *LH* deals with the story of Saint Catherine of Alexandria, the portion of the book that has received least textual and critical attention. It was last edited over a hundred years ago by Hermann Knust (see chapter VII, below). Catherine, an orphaned Christian, finds herself in opposition to the edict of the emperor Maxentius that all citizens must make sacrifice to the pagan gods. The story is a series of episodes in the crucial conflict or antagonism between Catherine and the emperor, ranging from religious disagreement to non-mutual sexual attraction. In his recent article dealing with the stories of women saints in medieval France, Karl D. Uitti presents a seven-part synopsis of the antagonism between Catherine and Maxentius, and I refer the interested reader to his illuminating analysis. My analysis will center on several key issues.

First, Catherine is presented as a woman of intelligence with superb knowledge of the liberal arts, the common curriculum of the Middle Ages: "Esta donzella pusiera su padre a ler de que fuera pequeña por aprender las artes./ & ella era tan bien enseñada / & tanto sabia./ que en aquel tiempo nonla podria ningunt maestro engañar por engeño de ssofismo" [fol. 15b]. She is able to muster her great learning with appropriate skill in disputation against fifty philosophers of the realm who have been called by the emperor to debate against her concerning the virtues of his pagan gods over her Christian one. At the end of the debate the "dean" of the learned gentlemen, confesses to the emperor:

> Entonçe Respondio vno dellos que todos tenjan por grant maestro & dixo al enperador./ enperador vna cosa te digo yo. Ante que esta donzella se tomase connosco a rrazonar non ouo tal denos que non toujese / que la vençeria muy toste / mas desto es otra cosa / & otra rrazon / muy longada de las otras./ & que te yo verdat quesiese dezir./ esta mugier non fabla por spiritu terenal./ mas çierta mente fabla ella por spiritu del çielo / que non semeja de ome mortal. [fol. 18c]

In fact, what the philosoper says is true. Earlier in the tale we have been told that an "angel del çielo" came to her to announce:

Donzella non ayas pauor ca a dios fazes plazer mas mantienete esforçada mente / ca nuestro señor es contigo por cuyo nonbre tu començaste esta batalla./ ca el abondada mente metera en tu boca la fuerça de su palabra / Asy que tus / auersarios non se poderan defender contra ty./ & todos seran vençidos / & cofondidos por vna manera despanto. [fol. 17a]

It is worth noting that Catherine emphatically and often conceives of herself as the spouse of Christ: "Jhesu xpisto me ha conquisa por esposa / & yo so junta a jhesu xpisto como esposa / por tal pleito que non puede desfecho ser njn desliado" [fol. 19b]. Earlier in the *LH* the Virgin had been praised as not only the mother of God, but also his daughter: ". . . el fue tu padre & tu fijo / & tu le fuste fija & madre . . ." [fol. 9c]. Now in this section Catherine takes on yet another familial role with Christ, that of his spouse. It is no wonder that the words of the angel quoted above have the ring of the "Ave Maria:" "nuestro señor es contigo. . . ."

However blessed by the Lord, Catherine's intelligence is not unique among the female protagonists of the *LH*, as we have already seen in our discussion of St. Martha. To mention three additional examples one might consider the spouse of King William in *La estoria del Rey Gujllelme*: "& la Reyña era muy sesuda . . ." [fol. 33b], the queen in *De vna santa enperatris*: "era muy fermosa & mucho enseñada" [fol. 100b] and the following description of Florençia in the *Otas* text:[8]

quando llego / a hedat de quinze años./ fue tan bella & tan cortes & tan bien enseñada / que en todo el mundo / nonle sabian par./ ya delas escripturas njn delas estoria njnguno non / sabia mas./ dela harpa & de viola & delos otros estromentos njnguno non fue mas maestre & con todo esto le diera dios tal donayre que non se abondauan las gentes de oyr su palabra. onde ella era mucho abondada & mucho conplida . . . [fols. 48d-49a]

As discussed above, earlier attempts to find unity in MS h.I.13 were based on seeing it as a collection of tales concerning pious women. This tale of Cataljna, however, teaches us that these are not just *pious* women, but more importantly, *learned* women, whose ed-

---

[8] Cristina González has discussed this same passage in *"Otas,"* 186-187.

ucation and expertise in many of the arts was hard won and, in the case of Cataljna, blessed by God in words very reminiscent of the "Ave Maria" in a situation that parallels the biblical Anunciation, a scene portrayed so often in the art of the ages that our pilgrim readers and hearers would have seen it all along the Via Lactea. Worthy of note is the fact that the *LH* presents the *imitatio Christi* or recapitulation of the life of Christ and his saints through female examples. In the discussion of Mary the Egyptian above we took note of the definition of a pilgrim as someone who is going to "visitar los santos & las santas" [fol. 100c]. Note how the text is insistent on going beyond the basic meaning that would have been conveyed by the masculine "los santos" by including the feminine and female term. This is one of the many ways the *LH* takes up the cause of women.

In fact, the *LH* must be seen in the light of the medieval debate concerning whether the nature of women is closer to that of the first sinner, Eve, or to that of the Virgin and intercessor without equal, Mary – the EVA/AVE[9] polemic or split. The *LH* actually in-

---

[9] Ave, the first word in Gabriel's annunciation to Mary and in the most common prayer to the Virgen (Hail Mary, full of grace . . . – in Latin, Ave Maria, gratia plena) clearly refers to Mary, the motherly mediatrix without equal. It is the palindrom of EVA, the first female, and for most medieval people the perpetrator of man's fall from grace. Fall and condemnation as well as mediation and salvation are available through females whose names and whose attributes are related in mirror image (See Chiara Frugoni, "The Imagined Woman," 336). See also Victor Yelverton Haines, *The Fortunate Fall*, Chapter 1 "The Felix Culpa" for details concerning the juxtaposition of Eve and Mary. Among other aspects, Haines states:

> The closeness of the annunciations to the First and Second Eve, the Virgin Eve and the Virgin Mary, was also underlined by the ninth-century hymn 'Ave maris stela,' in which the Latin 'Eva' is reversed to the 'Ave' of the annunciation: 'Sumens illud Ave/ Gabrielis ore,/ funda nos in pace,/ mutans nomen Evae' ('Receiving this Ave from the mouth of Gabriel, found us in peace reversing the name of Eve'.) The point of the reversal is not only the antithesis between Eve and Mary but also the witty one-way reversal so that from the source of our perdition comes salvation. In the glorious pairing of Eve and Mary, Eve is no longer hatefully rejected but becomes a necessary and paradoxically joyful part. (24-26)

Note that names have an essential relationship to the persons, objects, and things they denote. Or as Michael Camille has stated the situation:

> Power was embodied in the very naming of objects, for according to medieval epistemology, *vox significans rem*; there existed a real relationship between the sound of a word and its referent. According to St. Augustine, God 'spoke' the universe during the Creation, part of a strong phonocentric bias through which commentators expressed the force of the *Logos* in human society. ("Seeing and Reading" 30)

corporates this polemic into its structure by placing the story of Santa Maria Egiçiaca early in the collection. The story of the Egiçiaca, as we have seen, is one of a terribly lascivious sinner who cannot find full satisfaction for her carnal appetites. Her beauty drives males into frenzies and initiates a deadly series of sins in her and in others:

> Ella era muy fermosa asi como uos dixe / & deseauan la mucho / los mançebos dela tierra todo su cuydado era de bien comer & de bien beuer / & de ser sienpre en luxuria //. & los mançebos de la villa eran tan ençendidos en su amor. / que fazian mucho a menudo grandes peleas ante su puerta / por cobdiçia de la auer & ella que esto veya non fazia synon Reyr se / & non daua Ren sy se matasen todos. / que por vno que muriese venjan y dos & sy fuese llagado non lo catauan / njn ella dexaua por eso de se Reyr & ser leda. / [fol. 8a]

There could be no better example of the wiles of women and how they lead to death and destruction. This initial section of the tale of the Egiçiaca joins ranks with the misogynist tradition. However, as we have already seen, the tale takes Mary on a pilgrimage to the Holy Land, presents her miraculous conversion, her severe penance, and her exemplary status. Her moment of conversion is followed by a confession she makes (as the repulsive EVA) to an image of the Virgin, actually repeating the words of the "Ave Maria":

> señora Regna / Señora santa maria que en tu cuerpo troxiste tu padre & tu fijo / quando el angel graujel fue mensagero & dixote. / dios te salue maria / tu eres llena de graçia de dios el fijo de dios dela magestad que prendera humanidat enty / . . . [fol. 9b]

As we have seen, the image miraculously responds to the Egiçiaca and sends her to the desert to do penance. The text presents the transformation of EVA into AVE and in so doing ends on a pro-feminine note. [10]

---

[10] There is no doubt that the text leaves very little place in the lives of women for any activity other than sin or perfection, the virgin/whore dichotomy (See Beth Miller, 8). This lack of subtlety in dealing with females, and with the female protag-

In addition to having strong Marian elements throughout, the *LH* underscores the virtue, intelligence, perseverence, and stalwart strength of its female protagonists. In contrast to the better known misogynist texts of the Middle Ages (one thinks of the *Corbacho* of the Arcipreste de Talavera, for instance) where women are seen as the source of evil, the *LH* consistently shows males to be the source of lasciviously inappropriate and sinful behavior. An excellent example is Miles (or Millon), one of the beautiful twin brothers in *Otas*, who, caught in the snares of carnal desire and falling more and more deeply into a vortex of sin, treachery, and lies, is eventually punished with becoming a leper. Despite his initial physical beauty and military prowess [fol. 84b30-31], he is described as "falso" [fol. 57a]; shown to be envious of his younger twin brother [fol. 62b]; is portrayed as a liar [fols. 62c; 77b; etc.]; is accused of seeing other human beings as nothing more than merchandise – a medieval version of the objectification of females – showing him thus to have the lowly soul of a merchant [fol. 68a]. He becomes "endiablado" (a situation often seen as typical of females in misogynist literature) [fol. 81b31], and recognizes his own evil, yet is ineffectual in repenting:

> mucho era en grant cuydado & triste por la trayçion que auia fecha & dezia muchas vezes entre sy quando sele menbraua, Ay señor dios en mal punto fuy nasçido que trayçion fize a mj hermano que era Rey sagrado & coronado que era menor que yo & mejor verdadera mente el diablo entro en mj Ca fize como tredor prouado & sere por ende escarnido do quier que me fallen millon auia desto tan grant pesar que por poco se maldexiera . . . [fol. 84c2-15]

And, as pointed out above, he takes on an external sign of his internal corruption by becoming a leper [fol. 94a].

In the face of such unequivocal evidence concerning the character of Miles, the reader/hearer is presented with the irony of the

---

onists of the collection, has been noted by Cristina González for other texts of *LH*, see González ("Otas" and "*Vna santa*"). It seems clear to me that the limited roles allowed women in the text, despite its championing of them, has to do with the fact that they are texts *about* women not *by* women. In *The Lady as Saint*, Brigitte Cazelles speaks of some of the very saints we have studied: ". . . our saintly protagonists are 'locked into male texts' and, as such, into the construct of an authoritative male discourse on the proper place of women" (82).

false accusation he makes against Florençia, the innocent female, in his attempt to take revenge for the fact that she has rejected him sexually [fol. 77c]. [11] A similar situation obtains in *De vna santa enperatris* where the exemplary empress is left behind in Rome under the care of her brother-in-law while the emperor goes to the Holy Land on pilgrimage. The brother-in-law becomes overwhelmed by "la mala cobdiçia de su carne . . . que era vil cosa & mala" [fol. 101b] and exhibits all the signs of "follia" [fol. 101b] and "mal seso" [fol. 101d]. When he is unsuccessful in his carnal desires and is punished, he awaits the return of his brother and then falsely accuses the queen of the same behavior he himself wanted to pursue:

> Non fablan todos de al sinon della – fol en pleito, fol en palabra. A todos se abaldona a quantos la quieren asi a clerigos como a legos. que uos dire, mas tanta ha fecha de desonrra a uos & al coronado enperio que nunca uos deuedes con ella boluer en lecho tanto como fariades con vna Rapaza. . . . [fol. 104b]

One must ask if we are not to understand therefore that all such accusations must be understood in such a light, i. e. that the worst sinners, those who have what the codex calls "la lengua muy polida como fol" [fol. 107b], are those doing the accusation – a projection upon the contrasexual other of their own vile traits. As a third example, this time from the culminating story of the collection, *El noble cuento del enperador Carlos Maynes*, comes from near the end of the tale when the emperor Carlos Maynes is beseiged in the castle of Altafoja by the combined forces of his son Loys; Ricardo, the emperor of Greece; and the Apostoligo, the Pope of Rome. Carlos is advised by the faithful duque don Aymes that he should relent in his earlier decision to banish his wife and that in so doing he will avoid war and destruction and will achieve peace and harmony. Upon hearing this advice, Mançions, identified in the text as "un gran traidor" [fol. 144c], reminds the emperor of the sins of Seuilla, the empress, an accusation that has been a leitmotif running throughout the text in the mouths of the clan of traitors:

---

[11] See Schlauch for the classic discussion of the theme of the falsely accused queen.

> Señor dixo mançions vn gran traidor / Aquel dia que la uos
> tomardes / sea yo escarnido: / mugier que asi ando abaldonada /
> a quantos la querian por la tierra que non ouo garçon que non
> feziese enella ssu voluntad. [fol. 144c]

By this point in the tale, everyone except for Carlos Maynes
himself[12] is aware of the treachery of the clan of traitors ("los pa-
rientes de Galalon") and knows to beware of such misinformation.
Indeed, when the evil men talk in any of these texts their words
parallel the argumentation of the misogynist tradition, yet we, as
readers and hearers, know that the person talking, the male, is real-
ly the wicked, conniving traitor. The conclusion, then, is that the *LH*
enters the fray of the pro- versus anti-female debate intent on creating in its audience an almost automatic understanding that the accusations and insults made by males against females apply to the
males themselves.[13]

C.II. AN EXCURSUS ON *SESO/FOLLIA*

An aspect that gives greater impact to this irony is the presence
of the typical medieval contrast between *seso* and *cordura* on the
one hand and *follia* and *locura* on the other. Inevitably in these texts
the females are seen to be masters at logic and intelligence (i. e.
worldly knowledge) and to possess "seso," thus avoiding being a *fol*
or undertaking *follias;* that is, they possess prudence, spiritual
knowledge, and discernment. As we have seen above, the tone is set
by the text of the story of Santa Catalina in which the saint is depicted as a witty, silver-tongued public debater who from childhood
had excelled in learning: "Esta donzella pusiera su padre a ler . . ."

---

[12] See below, chapter IV.H, on *Carlos Maynes* and the gullibility of kings.

[13] Cristina González, in *"Otas,"* has analyzed this situation in the *LH* in a similar way. Her argument hinges on the difference between what is told and what is
shown:

> todas las . . . mujeres . . . que aparecen en estos relatos(,) son buenas,
> mientras que no sucede lo mismo con los hombres, muchos de los cuales
> son malos. Hay una contradicción entre *lo que se dice*, que parece dirigi-
> do al público masculino, y *lo que se muestra*, que parece dirigido al
> público femenino. *Lo que se dice* es que el mundo está lleno de mujeres
> peligrosas para los hombres, pero *lo que se muestra* es un mundo contro-
> lado por hombres peligrosos para las mujeres . . . (182)

etc. The story of Catalina involves her refusal to bow down and worship graven images and idols at the express command of the emperor Maxençio. She proceeds to tell him exactly why she will not do so, and the emperor is duly impressed both by her beauty and her wits and hopes to win her over to his side. As we have seen above, he sets up a debate with the philosophers of his realm in which Cataljna emerges the victor. The emperor then proceeds to imprison and torture Catalina. Eventually he will have to do the same with his wife who is won over by the virtuous virgin. As this development takes place, Catalina becomes fresher than a rose as the emperor Maxençio becomes more and more "brauo" [fol. 21a and elsewhere], "sañudo" [fol. 22d] and close to losing his mind "a pocas non ensandeçio" [fol. 22d].

The story of Catalina sets a pattern for the anthology in which heroine after heroine works hard to maintain her purity and avoid fornication and other sinful acts, thus following the will of the Lord and in so doing showing "buen seso" and "cordura," while the villainous men indulge themselves in unjust treachery and foolhardy acts of depravity (or allow others to do so) which inevitably lead them to death or to states of mental, physical, and spiritual disease – states described in terminology very similar to that used in the Catalina text (see page 125, 64-116 of *Santa enperatris* and fol. 149c of the *Carlos Maynes* text, for instance, and my comments in "Symbolic" 6-7).

The last comment to be made concerning the story of St. Catherine is that it is the tale that least exhibits the framework of elements related to pilgrims and pilgrimage. Yet in its championing the cause of female intelligence and by illustrating the ways in which females participate in the *imitatio Christi* it provides vital structural and thematic links for the compilers' project of conjoining the nine texts. With this said, let us hasten to point out that the tale does make at least some reference to pilgrimage. In answer to a question from Porfiro, one of her new converts from paganism, concerning the reward Christians will have for their suffering in this life, Cataljna answers:

> & la bendita virgen dixo porfiro entiendeme /. este mundo es asy como vna carçel muy escura & eneste mundo non ha ninguno que non muera /. mas enla çelestial tierra por que ome despreçia el mundo es vna çibdat enque sienpre ha sol enque ningunt

pesar non ha ome njn ningunt trabajo mas perdurable bona an-
dança & alegria sin fin. [fol. 20b]

Cataljna understands that this world is not our real home, but a
road to the other *patria* or fatherland since she, like all Christians,
knows that we all dwell as pilgrims in a mutable world that will give
way to unchanging truth and reality on Judgment Day.

D. El Cauallero Plaçidas

The next story included in the *LH* is the legend of the knight
Plaçidas or St Eustace, an up-dated Job story on the theme of the
"man tried by fate." Plaçidas, a Roman general, goes out to hunt
and encounters a stag from whose antlers comes forth the voice of
the Lord instructing him first to seek baptism, and then to keep the
faith as he is tried by a series of losses, hardships and setbacks. He
is assured that should he keep the faith, he will eventually be rewarded with "Riquezas çelestiales" [fol. 25c]. Indeed, the Lord,
who is the "enperador del perdurable jnperyo" [fol. 25d] assures
him in the following words: "fazer te he cobrar toda tu primera
onrra / & tu primero plazer & despues darte la alegria del
paraiso:/" [fol. 25d].

The hardships brought upon Plaçidas are numerous, including
the death of his retainers and his livestock. He decides to leave his
home taking his family with him, and the empty house is robbed by
the neighbors. Later he seeks passage to Egypt and must give up his
wife as price for the passage to a person Teospita, his wife, will later
describe as "el mal marjnero" [fol. 29d]. This is the first appearance of such a character type that will be presented in an increas-
ingly sinister way in the next two tales. As Plaçidas flees with his
two sons he looses them at a river crossing, one to a lion and the
other to a wolf. The *Plaçidas* story is the first in the *LH* in which
there is a situation of family separation and eventual reunion.

Plaçidas himself is finally taken in by a village and he becomes
the overseer of the vineyards and other endeavors of the area. He is
missed by the emperor, who is lacking his prowess at war, and by
several of his Roman friends who seek approval from the emperor
for a search expedition. They come upon the town where Plaçidas
is working and the three eventually recognize one another. Plaçidas

recovers his former station in life, and in an army campaign he comes upon and is reunited with his wife and children in a series of what seem to be implausible coincidences. The family is reinstated in Rome, but is eventually martyred in a brass oven for refusing to sacrifice to the pagan gods.

There are several elements in the narrative that are worthy of our interest in elucidating the elements common to the tales of the *LH*. The Plaçidas tale is the first in the book which utilizes the situation of family separation and reunion. It is my belief that the pilgrim reader/hearer would understand the situation of the separated and exiled characters as symbolic pilgrims. Note that when Plaçidas decides to take leave of his home he says: "partamos nos de aqui / ca todos nos despreçian quantos nos conosçen / Tanto que fue noche tomaron sus fijos / & fueron se contra egipto . . ." [fol. 26b]. One is reminded of the flight of the Holy Family into Egypt, one of the biblical episodes commonly seen as a pilgrimage. In addition, once he has lost his family, Plaçidas makes an assessment of his situation in which he compares his own situation to Job's. In this assessment he say of himself: "yo so en tierra estraña" and "yo ando solo por el yermo entre bestias fieras . . ." [fol. 27a]. Note the presence in these statements of several of the "cluster of keywords" associated with pilgrimage.

More telling, however, are two recognition scenes woven into the story which mirror the Emmaus tale. First we have the recognition scene between the exiled Plaçidas and two friends from his former life who requested permission from the emperor to search for their missing friend. They come upon the village where Plaçidas has been given refuge (hospice?) and he recognizes them almost immediately, although the situation is not mutual: "& quanto se mas llego / a ellos tanto los conosçio mejor./ mas ellos nonlo conosçieron . . ." [fol. 28a]. They ask him if he has seen "vn ome estraño" by the name of Plaçidas. He answers in the negative, but presses hospice upon these men. The text is worth quoting at length:

> Non vy dixo el aqui tal ome njnlo conosçy./ pero yd oy comigo albergar./ ca yo otrosy so de tierra estraña/; Entonçe los leuo consigo asu posada/ & fue corriendo por vjno que les diese a beuer./ ca mucho fazia grant calentura / & dixo aun su buen huespede con que posaua./ Amigo/ yo coñosco estos omes anbos / & por esto los troxe aca / & Ruego vos que me enprestedes

vjno / & lo al que oujer menester por que los pueda / tener
viçiosos./ . . . & el huesped le enpresto de grado quanto / ouo
menester./ . . . sant eustaçio non se podia sofrir de llorar / por
que le nenbraua de su primera vida & saliose fuera de casa / &
lloro muy fyera mente / & desque lloro mucho lauo su faz / &
torno a casa & serujo los caualleros./ & los caualleros lo cataron
/ & Recataron / & fueron lo conosçiendo poco a poco / dixo el
vno en poridat al otro:/ mucho me semeja este ome aquel que
nos demandamos./ verdadera mente dixo el otro / nunca vy cosa
que mas me semejase./ [By means of a scar they are able to identify Plaçidas.] & preguntaronle en llorando Señor sodes uos el
maestre delos caualleros del enperador./ & el en llorando otrosy
dixo non. / non dixieron ellos ca uos vemos el señal dela cabeça
por que uos conosçemos / & como quier que el negase jurauan
ellos que aquel era / plaçidas el cauallero / cabdillo de los
caualleros./ & ellos le preguntaron por su mugier / & por sus
fijos & por otras muchas cosas:/ & sant eustaçio seles fizo entonçe coñosçer . . . [fols. 28b-c]

He insists that they spend the night with him (albergar), thus press-
ing hospice upon them while he, in turn, is overwhelmed with emotions dealing with the remembrance of his former life–a counterpart to when the Emmaus travelers felt their hearts burn within
their breasts. Note that here our exiled protagonist, a guest himself,
plays the role of host, thus combining in a single character the two
roles involved in guest/host theology.

The story quickly presents another recognition scene which
likewise possesses aspects of the Gregorian pattern of pilgrimage. It
is when the two sons have been recruited to serve in the very army
that Plaçidas commands in his now reinstated status. The army has
come to the town where Teospita, the wife of Plaçidas and the
mother of the boys, has found refuge. The boys are billeted in her
hut and they begin to talk of their lives. As the one speaks, the
other boy recognizes his brother, as does the mother. She goes to
request of the Roman commander that she be taken back to Rome
since she is a Roman citizen at which point she recognizes him as
her missing husband by means of a scar – Frye's "talisman of recognition" (see Liffen 15). The reunion is complete when she tells him
that his sons, too, are safe and near at hand. She reports to him how
the boys told each other their stories and recognized each other in
their tales: "todas las cosas contaron / & en su cuento fallaron-

se por hermanos" [fol. 30b]. Can there be a better example of
Gardiner's characterization of the Gregorian pattern of pilgrimage:
". . . the human exile finds the celestial home *in men and their
words* . . ." (19) [my emphasis].

Finally, it is worth pondering the martyrdom of the family in a
brass oven from the perspective of a pilgrim walking to Santiago.
Every pilgrim knows there are days on the plains of Castile and
Leon when the heat is such that all compare it to an oven. Heat, of
course, is only one of the many hardships of daily walking. Would
the medieval pilgrim reader/hearer, then, not see a parallel between
his/her own travails of heat, etc. and those of these saints of earlier
days (*in illo tempore*)? Is not the oft-repeated schema of the "tres
njños de baujloña" (see above, chapter III.F) intended precisely to
reinforce such ponderings? It seems clear to me that all walking pilgrims would understand in a very personal way the "boz del çielo"
that comforts Plaçidas/Eustaçio in this ultimate trial by assuring
him that his worldly travails and woes will win for him the rewards
of Heaven: "vos aueredes por lloro lediçia / & por lazeria / viçio &'
por el pesar que Resçebiestes enel mundo aueredes grant plazer
enel paraiso" [fols. 31c-d]. My contention is that the compilers of
the *LH* intended just such a comparison and that it formed part of
their program of creating a pilgrim community that saw itself as a
new generation of sacred workers.

E. EL REY GUJLLELME

The next story, *La estoria del Rey gujllelme*, plays a pivotal role
in the structure of the *LH* since it tells a story that repeats the plot
of the saintly life of Plaçidas but is the first romance in the collection. As Liffen points out in the summary of her article:

> El otro aspecto de interés en ambos relatos radica en su situación
> central en el códice. Colocados entre cuatro narraciones de vidas
> de santas (Santa María Magdalena, Santa Marta, Santa María
> Egipciaca y Santa Catalina) y tres versiones del tema folclórico
> de la Reina Injustamente Acusada, estos dos relatos, en los que el
> héroe se parece a un Job medieval, proporcionan el eje de lo que
> – aparentemente – quiso mostrar el compilador del códice: una
> trayectoria desde la hagiografía hasta la novela en embrión. (16)

Although I think it odd to claim that the compiler (I imagine a group of compilers) intended by means of some form of telepathy to demonstrate the future literary development of the modern novel, I do agree with Liffen that the *Guijllelme* text glances back at the saints' lives just presented, including a repetition in plot of the most recent tale (*Plaçidas*), while also providing a foretaste of the stories to come, along with the issues and interests that will predominate in them. It is true that the *Gujllelme* and the tales that follow are romances, as has long been acknowledged by scholars. We as modern readers find romances more satisfactory experiences in terms of character development, psychological insight, etc. However, I cannot imagine that the average medieval reader/hearer had any concept of having shifted from one genre to another.[14] It is true that for the contemporary reader the romances show "greater complexity of character portrayal" (14), to use Liffen's words, but for medieval people I think a more accurate account of what they noticed would be along the lines traced by John Maier and myself where we pointed out that the romances lacked saints as characters and sometimes miracles as events – what we called "the external reference of the God without" (Maier/Spaccarelli 25). Without this reference the characters had to depend on faith and on what we called "reference to the God within" (*ibid.*). In this sense the characters presented in the romances are more like *real* medieval people. Most medieval people did not get to see God nor did they experience any supernatural proof of divine power, instead, they had to depend on faith and ritual. I would suggest that the intention of the compilers had little to do with Liffen's "stylistic subtlety" and "complexity of character" and more to do with the ideological and spiritual messages they intended to convey. The secularization of the stories has to do with the pattern or process of *imitatio Christi*, as discussed above, with the texts that we call romances providing a middle step leading to the last phase of the process, the one in which the pilgrim readers and hearers would consider themselves as rightful followers and heirs in the trajectory of saints, hero-

---

[14] I offer as only one piece of evidence the fact that the beginnings of both hagiographic tale and romance make an effort to base the stories they will narrate on historical fact. The tale of St. Catherine begins: "Las estorias nos enseñan . . ." [fol. 14c] and the "romance" of King William commences with the following words: "Dizen las estorias de ynglaterra . . ." [fol. 32a].

ines, and heroes traced in the *LH*. It is in this sense that the *Gujl-lelme* text is a transitional piece. Brigitte Cazelles has used the term "hagiographic romance" in discussing a series of Old French saints' lives from the thirteenth century. She writes:

> In rewriting the hagiographic accounts transmitted by the Latin tradition, they drew their themes and techniques of composition from secular literature, twelfth-century courtly romance in particular, since the genre was then the most popular mode of literary expression. Resulting from the interaction between secular and saintly narratives in the thirteenth century, our textual corpus marks the flourishing of hagiographic romance. (8)

Noteworthy is the fact that within the corpus Cazelles mentions there are two of the tales that appear in the *LH*. John R. Maier in "Sainthood, Heroism" has used the term "secular hagiography" (424), borrowing a phrase from Diana Childress, and he claims that "the boundaries which seem to separate the two genres . . . come to be seen as less obvious and rather more opaque" (425). As Sheila Delany points out: "Hagiography itself is a deeply syncretic genre, over the centuries incorporating oriental and western folktale, classical myth and legend, adventure story, political propaganda, biography, travel literature, and romance" (xxii). One must also consult the evidence provided by John K. Walsh in "Chivalric Dragon" whenever considering the connections between hagiography and chivalric romance.

In the story of Gujllelme, God's messenger tells the King and his wife, Graçiana, that they should leave their kingdom and go into exile: "yo te so mandadero dela parte de dios que te vayas en este-rramiento & por que tanto tardas / este dios ya sañudo" [fol. 33a]. This demand seems to be in retribution for what William's chaplain calls the "muchas cosas syn derecho" [fol. 32c] that the king had done. William and Graçiana do leave the kingdom and go off through the *floresta* to their exile. It should be noted that Graçiana is pregnant at this moment. Again, I believe we have a reflection of Mary and Joseph going off first to Bethlehem and then to Egypt, stories associated with pilgrimage. The queen gives birth to twin boys and the king cuts his cloak (*garnacha*) in two in order to provide bedding and wraps for the infants.

Next we have the separation episode in which Graçiana is forcibly taken by a group of merchants. Gujllelme must allow this event to transpire since he is horribly outnumbered: "viose tan solo que se non oso tomar con ellos" [fol. 35a]. In short order he looses both of the male children that had been born to Graçiana, one to a wolf and another abandoned in a boat. The children are found by *mercaderos* who wish to take them in as their own and the infants are given the names of Lobel (Lobato) and Maryn according to the situations in which they were found.

The king and queen both find reasonable positions in which they spend their exile, he as the overseer for a merchant, the "burges de galuoya," she "by accepting a *mariage blanc*" (Liffen 14) with an elderly landowner. It is interesting that the queen tries to avoid this relationship by accusing herself of a fictitious past that parallels in lasciviousness and depravity the early life of Mary the Egyptian: "& fiz mala vida andando por las tierras.// asi como mugier mala auenturada./ & mal acostunbrada / & abaldonada / a quantos me querian" [fol. 37b]. This false self incrimination is similar to the false accusations hurled at several of the queens in the romances that occur later in the *LH*, words that will ring even more false to those readers and hearers of this earlier tale. Curiously, the elderly man is unmoved and claims that much good can come of evil. He intends to marry her despite her background: "& ya por pecado njn por al / non uos dexare de tomar por mugier:/ Non sabedes uos que la castaña es dulçe & sabrosa pero sale del orizo espinoso yo non se sy vuestro / padre fue Rey o enperador / mas muchos malos salen de buenos, & muchos buenos de malos" [*ibid.*]. We should keep this dictum in mind as we look at the next issue to be presented in the text.

The two boys are taken and raised by their *mercadero* foster fathers. By the time they are twelve they have taken on exceptional qualities: "non podria ome enel mundo fallar mas fermosos dos njños / mejor enseñados:/ & esto les venja por derecha natura" [fol. 38b]. The text takes pains to develop what can be called a doctrine of *natura*, which is none other than a type of biological imperative that insists that goodness comes through one's lineage:

> esto les venja por derecha natura / que vençe criazon & jamas non falleçe./ ca natura es dulçe & amargosa / vna es toruada./ otra es llana / vna es bieja / otra es Nueua tal como natura es enel ome:/ tal es el ome & esta es la çima./ ca tan grant fuerça / a la natura que ella faz el ome bueno / o malo / & sy natura se

pudiese canbiar./ los Niños que eran criados / de dos villanos
non podrian ser tan buenos./ mas la buena natura donde venja
los fazia ser tan buenos & tan bien enseñados / & los fazia
guardar de yerro:/ asy que non podian salir ala criança delos
males tanto eran de grant ljnaje. [fol. 38b]

The text tells of the interest the foster fathers have concerning how
the young men should make a living. They suggest that the boys
take up the profession of "pelliteria" [fol. 38c], an idea the boys reject claiming that neither will do anything without the companionship of the other. The two fathers become angry, each striking his
respective ward. Frochel, the foster father of Marin, calls his son
"rrapaz & fijo de puta" [*ibid.*]. The text comments: "Agora se
prouo el villano por qual era ora prouo bien su natura./ maldita sea
la lengua del villano / maldito sea su coraçon:/ maldita sea su boca"
[*ibid.*]. The young men decide that they must withdraw from this
situation and decide to take their leave of these foster fathers. Lobato bids farewell to his foster father, Gloçelins, from whom he has
received better treatment than did Marin from his father Frochel.
He says to the man: ". . . diestes me vida ca me tolliestes al lobo./ &
pues me le tolliestes./ lo que yo bjuo / & lo que yo so./ por vos es:/
& non poderia padre / mas fazer por fijo / & por ende sabed que
toda via sere vuestro do quier que yo sea . . ." [fol. 39a]. Frochel in
turn apologizes to Maryn for his anger and claims that it was an expression of his desire to teach the child for his own good: ". . . per-
donar me deues ca estaua sañudo / tu non eres mal traydo de cosa
que te yo dixiese / njn feziese / ca por tu pro telo fazia" [fol. 39a].
In addition, he tells his son to seek wealth because the world is such
that:

> el que es Rico muchos amigos falla./ & mucho es vil el que non
> ha nada . . . Ca oy es el dia en que el sesudo / sy pobre fuer en
> toda corte lo ternan por torpe / & el torpe sy fuer rrico por sesu-
> do./ el costunbre dela tierra este es Por ende te consejo / que
> ayas auer en qual quier guisa que pudieres sy quesieres ser onrra-
> do / & semejar sesudo eneste sieglo. [fols. 39a-b]

The text says that "de todo esto non ouo el moço cura./ ca su natura gelo defendia" [fol. 39b], suggesting that the desire for wealth is
not seemly in the highborn. The boy sets off at that point, concerned that his close friend Maryn is not with him. However, there

is a happy meeting on the road and the two young men wander off to encounter soon thereafter the King of Catanassa who takes them in as wards and has them trained as knights by one of his *monteros*:

> Toma estos njños / & guarda & piensa me dellos muy bien / & dales canes & aues & enseñalos & lieualos contigo a monte & a Ribera cada que fueses a caçar . . . & los njños cayeron en tan grant amor conel Rey / que el Rey les mando dar que vistiesen & quitaçiones asu voluntad: / & fazia los yr consigo sienpre a monte por caçar. [fol. 40c]

The doctrine of *natura,* a reflection of the hierarchical reality of the Middle Ages, represents what Liffen calls a "romantic sense of caste" (14) and what Frye calls the "pervasive social snobbery" of romance" (161). It appears to argue against the egalitarianism I claim exists in the *LH.* This is particularly the case if one looks at the *Gujllelme* text alone and in isolation–the way in which the consituent texts of the *LH* have been commonly read and studied. However, in the context of the *LH*'s other tales, this doctrine of *natura* and both its "sense of caste" and its "social snobbery" can be seen in a different light. That different light is the schizophrenic nature of the collection as described by Cristina González in "Vna santa enperatriz: novela esquizofrénica," one of the most perceptive pieces written about the *LH.* González believes the collection to be a "libro de texto para educar a las mujeres que es, a la vez, una obra de propaganda para reclutar monjas . . ." (165) which uses "procedimientos esquizofrénicos" (*ibid.*) by saying one thing and showing another. She states: "Se trata de una novela esquizofrénica, que adopta la forma del sermón para decir algo diferente, aunque complementario, a lo que muestra en el ejemplo" (161). [15] I believe the same thing can be said of the doctrine of *natura* as presented in the *Gujllelme* text – the doctrine tells us one thing, but the text shows us something else.

Let us look first at where in the *Gujllelme* text itself we might find it showing us something different. At the end of the tale, when the royal family has been reinstated to its power and rightful positions, the foster fathers are called to court in order to receive their

---

[15] González has used a similar argument in analyzing the male/female axis of the text. See above, chapter IV.C, "De santa cataljna...," p. 62, note 10.

rewards for having provided hospice to the infants Lobel and
Maryn. Lobel tells their story to the assembled *cortes*: "destos omes
buenos que aqui vedes / fumos nos / sanos & saluos . . . & jamas
contra nos non oujeron pan so llaue" [fol. 46c]. This is a repetition
of an earlier statement put in the mouths of the two boys:

> mas con todo esto non deuemos oluidar los mercaderos que nos
> criaron / njn el bien que nos fezieron./ & njngunt debdo non
> aujan conusco por que / & derecho es que los veamos sy quier
> que sepan lo que fallaron & quien denostaron./ & que ayan
> denos del bien que nos fezieron gualardon ssy dios a tienpo nos
> llega. [fol. 45c]

It is clear that the two *mercaderos* fulfilled the role of hosts with
generosity; they are rewarded by being clothed in rich cloth which
they, as merchants, would gladly sell for profit. The queen takes
great pleasure in their "plebeian" merchant's attitude and the text
makes fun of the men since they allow the queen to buy back her
gifts to them and then to give them again. It assures us that "su
donayro era tan vil / & tan mal se vistian dellos que semejaua / que
los trayan enprestados de otri" [fol. 47a]. The conclusion would
seem clear: the clothes of the powerful and worthy fit badly on the
lowborn. The only problem is that the story is very clear in reporting that the "worthy," cultured folk have survived because of the
actions and work of the lowborn. The reader is left at this point
pondering the incongruency of the upper-class mocking the very
people responsible for its survival. Perhaps a better understanding
of the situation is that what occurs is not mockery, but good humor.
Earlier in the tale the queen had showed a sense of humor in an
episode with King William (see below, this section). Also, not many
folios before this clothing episode it is mentioned that Lobel and
Maryn had fought against their mother in the war the King of
Catanassa had waged against her in an effort to make her marry
him. It is King William himself who states: "& sy sus fijos vos ayu-
daron contra ella./ fezieron derecho ca los criastes./ mas non lo
fezieran / si su madre conosciesen / ca mala mente yerra / quien
toma guerra contra su madre" [fols. 45b-c]. The moral paradox is
made clear at the end of his statement: "& asy en vn meesmo
seruiçio eran leales & desleales & fazian bien & mal./ mas non
deuen ser por ende culpados ca, lo vno,./ o lo otro les convenja

fazer: /" [fol. 45c]. We can conclude that the royal sons are no more contradictory than their lowborn *huespedes*, who, if laughed at in court, are also included among the most prestigious in the realm in a list at the end of the tale where they are accorded the honorific title of "don" [fol. 47b].

In subsequent parts of the collection, in texts that parallel many aspects of the *Gujllelme* text, there are passages and situations that warn against accepting the doctrine of *natura* at face value. What are these passages and situations? First let us mention the very next story in the *LH*, the *Cuento del enperador Otas de Roma*. In this tale twin brothers are wandering in search of a new home because of the death of their father and the remarriage of their mother to an evil step-father. These twins (are we not to think back on Lobel and Maryn?) come to the defense of Otas and his daughter Florençia against the foolish and agressive Garssir. Both Esmere and Miles are skilled knights capable of great prowess, and, as twins, share the same lineage. Yet as the story unfolds, Esmere, the younger of the two brothers, emerges as a worthy hero whereas Miles, his elder brother, plumbs the depths of depravity and madness (see above, chapter IV.C, pp. 63-64, for a more detailed discussion of Miles). How does the doctrine of *natura* apply here? What accounts for the depravity of one brother and the heroism of the other? The text makes it clear that Miles is *endiablado*. That is to say, his dastardly acts are not the product of his birth, but rather the product of low moral standards. He chooses to be evil; his actions are not determined by his social status.

In the last story of the collection, the culminating *Cuento del enperador Carlos Maynes,* there is a low-born host/pilgrim character (called *villano* in the text, as were Frochel and Gloçelins in the *Gujllelme* text) who emerges as a generous foster father and as a protector to two of the main characters, the falsely accused queen Seuilla and Loys, her son by Charlemagne. At one point Barroquer (the name of the *villano* in question) goes off in pilgrim garb to see his wife and on his sojourn (a type of pilgrimage) he happens upon Carlos Maynes, the husband of his beloved Seuilla and father to his stepson, Loys. Carlos Maynes as depicted in the tale is a gullible, easily deceived monarch who is under the influence of a clan of evil nobles. By means of great cleverness Barroquer is able to steal the king's favorite steed, which he rides wielding his pilgrim's staff as if it were a knight's lance: ". . . metio el bordon so el braço derecho /

& conlos grandes çapatos que tenja Aguyjo el cauallo & soltole la Rienda & el cauallo començo de correr tan fiera mente que seme-jaua que bolaua . . ." [fol. 145b]. In exchange he leaves for the monarch his own pilgrim's cloak. In an earlier study ("Symbolic") I pointed out that:

> As he leaves he calls back to the king, 'Rey, yo sso Barroquer de la barba cana . . . Este buen cauallo leuare yo & finque uos la mj esclauina, ca bien la auedes conprada.' . . . The low-born Barro-quer, who has proved to be noble in both action and thought, rides off on the emperor's horse and he leaves his humble [pil-grim's] cloak in exchange, thus suggesting that Carlos should set off on a common pilgrimage . . . in which he too might be reas-sured about Seuilla's chastity and fidelity, and relearn the impor-tance of family. (9)

At that specific point in the story it is not clear whether the worthy (but common) pilgrim's cloak will fit well on the gullible and emo-tionally distraught king. Note that the text presents here the mirror image or opposite of the clothing situation presented in the *Gujl-lelme,* and yet another example of a commoner (*villano*) who per-forms honorable deeds in a society where many of the nobles fail at even the most common decencies. In the text, Barroquer character-izes Charlemagne's banishment of Seuilla as "la villanja que el Rey contra vos fizo" [fol. 140b]. As I have indicated in "Symbolic": "the contrast here is significant: Carlos, the highest of nobles, is ac-cused of such a 'common' act, a *villanja,* by Barroquer the *villano,* whose actions and thoughts are consistently 'noble'" (8). I believe these issues are clear, both to us as contemporary readers, and, more importantly, also to the pilgrim readers and hearers of the Middle Ages.

 In conclusion, then, concerning the doctrine of *natura,* I believe the *LH* uses the doctrine as a ruse in the sense that by means of pre-senting it the text remains within the orthodox social and spiritual boundaries of its times thus avoiding censure, persecution, or worse. That is, the text *tells* us the hierarchical, biologically deter-mined doctrine of *natura* while it *shows* us the opposite of the doc-trine in case after case. To the late twentieth-century reader this would make for a schizophrenic text. To the pilgrim reader/hearer on the Road to Santiago it provided another example of a show/tell structural principle that can be observed in many of the texts of the collection. Anita Benaim de Lasry has shown how the last three tales of the *LH*, the *Otas*, *Santa enperatris*, and *Carlos Maynes* texts use "the contrast between female nobility and the bleak, conventional wisdom of the [period's] *sententiae* . . . [as] one of the most important and neglected narrative devices in the fourteenth-century Spanish romance" ("Narrative Devices" 281). She lists the various proverbs and *sententiae* of the period concerning the moral frailty and untrustworthy nature of females. In all three romances studied "the conduct of the heroines . . . demonstrates the very opposite" (*ibid.*) of what the conventional wisdom would have us believe concerning females. In its treatment of the doctrine of *natura*, then, the *Gujllelme* text joins the other romances of the collection in utilizing this contrastive, show/tell structural principle.[16]

There are several noteworthy recognition scenes in the *Gujllelme* that repeat elements we have already seen in the tale of Plaçidas. The king and queen are reunited after more than twenty years of separation and exile when the king appears in her city as the chief of a merchant vessel. She has the privilege of having her pick of the merchandise, and when she arrives at the ship, with her face hidden behind a veil, she sees her husband's hunting horn (a talisman of recognition) and then sees a ring on his finger that she had given to him (a second talisman), thus realizing that he is her husband. Of all the merchandise on the ship she desires the ring, which she playfully asks for and which the king finally gives to her after making every attempt to dissuade her: "mas pues el anjllo queredes tomaldo// & sabed que uos do muy grant don / & quelo saco de mj corasçon muy syn mj grado. ca en mj dedo nonlo tenja yo/ ora uos dj mj vida . . ."[fols. 43b-c]. In return for the ring she offers him hospice in her castle where the culminating recognition scene between them takes place during a meal: "&ntonçe lauaron se / & asentaron se alas mesas./ & la dueña fizo ser su huespede cabo sy a par & comieron anbos / & el cato a ella./ & ella a el asy que el conosçio que aquella era su mugier./ & syn falla aquella era . . ."

---

[16] Several characters are developed in a way that parallels this show/tell structure. Clarenbaut, the lying thief saved from the gallows by Florençia in the *Otas* tale, outwardly swears perpetual allegiance to Florençia despite his evil intentions. The text reports his words as follows: "Yo sso su ome quito & hele jurado quele non fallesca en toda mj vida. / Mas como quier quelo dezia por la boca non lo tenja asi enla voluntad . . ." [fols. 89b-c].

[fol. 43d]. The recognition at table fits well the "Gregorian pattern of pilgrimage" thus reinforcing our interpretation of these separations and exiles as a form of pilgrimage. One must also note the touch of humor in the queen's personality, an aspect we have already seen in the episode of the gifts of cloth to the foster fathers of Lobel and Maryn.

Earlier in the tale the king had recovered his horn when in England at a fair he ran into a boy who was selling it. Upon recognizing the object as his own he asks the young man how he came to possess it. The boy responds with a story about the time when King William had left the country: "las gentes dela villa fueron a su casa & rrobaronla./ & desque fue rrobada./ mety me yo so vn lecho / & falle este cuerno" [fol. 41b]. He has kept it safe up to this point, but now "quiero me yr en Romeria / a sant gil./ & andaua vendiendo el cuerno por dar los djneros a pobres por alma de mjo señor:/ & el Rey dixo bien feziste / cuydo quete verna avn dende bien./ avn alguno verna que telo gualardonara que agora tu non cuydas . . . " [*ibid.*]. It is significant that the horn was recovered by the king in a context of pilgrimage and generosity.

The scenes of recognition continue when King William goes out to hunt while a guest in the castle of his now recovered wife. She warns him that he should not cross a certain frontier, which he procedes to do. At that point he is attacked by the guardians of the wood, two young men who protect it for their patron, the King of Catanassa, who wages war against Graçiana in order to force her into marriage. These two young knights are about to kill King William when he warns them: "mal fecho queredes fazer en matar vn Rey . . ." [fol. 44d]. They question him as to this title and he procedes to tell them his story, including the separation from his wife and the loss of his two sons to a wolf and to the water current, at which point the sons realize that they are the man's sons while simultaneously recognizing their identity as brothers. Of course, in their hearts they had already known each other as spiritual brothers through the warmth of friendship; now they know the truth intellectually. This is surely a rendition of the "Gregorian pattern." The recognition is accompanied by talismans in the mentioning of the pieces of the king's *garnacha* that had been parted at their birth in order to give each twin a wrap. The interpretation of this scene as fitting into the "Gregorian pattern" is fortified when the two young men return to the king of Catanassa in order to tell him of their good fortune in finding their father. Both the king and the father are spoken of as *huespedes*, with the king being the "host" and the father being the "guest." "& tanto fezieron grant alegria que el huespede dixo bolsa auedes fallada./ verdat dezides dixo lobel / ca nos fallamos huesped nueuo en vuestra casa que nos deujamos mucho onrrar . . ." [fol. 45a].

The story of King William comes to an end when the royal family is reinstated to its rightful position and all the various *huespedes* are given their rewards: the *burges de galuoya* is made the king's *priuado*, and the pilgrim to San Gil, "el njño quel cuerno le vendiera enla feria de bretol" [fol. 48a] is given a yearly stipend of one hundred marks.

F. OTAS DE ROMA

The *Otas* story by virtue of its length (more that 51 of the 152 folios of the codex) is arguably the most important tale in the collection. González ("Otas" 188-189) considers the text of importance in the collection basing herself not on length but on the independent strength and joy of Florençia, the tale's main character, and on the "toque optimista" and "nota romántica" (189) that this secular, martial romance provides as an antidote to the other more pessimistic stories. She also points out that the tale combines the motif of the falsely accused woman with the motif of the heroic savior. As usual, González' analysis is tightly structured and insightful. *Otas de Roma* is the tale in the *LH* which is most chivalric in terms of the delight it takes in long, detailed, colorful descriptions of battles, battle gear and gore, and accoutrements (so plentiful that specific references seem pointless) and in its use of the structure of interlace which lends to it a repetitive (some might say monotonous) yet textured vista. (I think here of the repeated motif of false accusations by evil and rebuffed male suitors that is woven into the fabric of the tale at regular intervals – see analysis below.)

The tale deals with Otas, the emperor of Rome, and his daughter, Florençia. Garssir, the elderly emperor of Constantinople, makes war on Otas who has refused Garssir in his overtures of marriage to Florençia. In the early stages of Garssir's invasion of Rome it seems he will achieve victory when there arrive on the scene the heroic saviors, the twins Esmere and Miles. Esmere emerges as the true savior and takes Florença's hand in marriage at the death in battle of her father, Otas. He departs the realm in pursuit of the defeated Garssir, giving Miles an opportunity to show his jealousy of his brother (as first born he believes he has more rights than Esmere). Miles also emerges as an evil, adulterous, and conniving traitor and suitor to Florença. When he cannot have his way with her he abducts her, beats her, and leaves her for dead. He is unable to take her sexually because of a magic charm which protects her. Florença must wander from *huesped* to *huesped* since in each situation she is betrayed by evil males who are unable to requite their carnal lust for her. Her final refuge is in a monastery where she takes on great fame as a healer of lepers and other diseased persons. The four males who have caused her such travail (Miles, Escot, Macaire, and Clarenbaut) all fall ill with leprosy and, having heard of the miracle working nun, coincide at the monastery in search of a cure. Esmere also arrives in search of a cure for a fatal battle wound. Cures cannot be had without complete and public confession, which causes each of the culprits to relate the evil he perpetrated against the innocent empress. Esmere is healed and the four culprits are condemned to death. At the end of the tale Florença and Esmere have a son, Otas de Espoliça, the promise of a new generation of spiritual heroes.

The *Otas* story has already been discussed (pp. 63-65) as it relates to the issues of female intelligence, misogyny, and lascivious male characters with the example of Miles and his false accusation of Florença. In addition, it presents a case of family separation that can be construed as a symbolic pilgrimage. Furthermore, much of the suffering of the main character, Florença, can be understood in terms of *imitatio Christi*. The *Otas* is important, then, in the *LH* since it carries forward these themes and motifs of earlier tales while presenting for the first time several issues that will come to have importance as the book develops.

Let us look first at those elements of earlier stories that the *Otas* continues and which we have not yet discussed. Family separation occurs as a result of the kidnapping of Florença by Miles in an effort to force a sexual response from her. He is shown throughout the text as a jealous, deceitful individual, who is willing to betray both his brother and his sister-in-law whenever it suits his lust for sex and power. Despite his being caught at these activities, and put in prison, Florença shows clemency towards him, thus allowing him the freedom to betray and kidnap her. His attitude is such that since he cannot have her legitimately he will have her by force. This leads to the passage of the story that has received, perhaps, the most critical attention since according to some critics its French source is also a source for the Corpes episode in the *Poema de mio Cid* (see Walker, "Source"). Walker has understood well the psychology of Miles when he depicts him as "mentally sick," and "criminally insane" while suffering from an "inferiority complex" (341). These are the qualities of personality that allow him to kill a hermit and beat his sister-in-law with impunity. We should note that Florençia's suffering in these scenes is cast in terms of the *imitatio Christi*. First, her suffering occurs over three days, reminiscent of the period Jonah spent in the belly of the whale, and, more importantly, of the period after the crucifixion in which Jesus descended into hell to conquer the forces of evil and death. In describing her situation to the hermit, she states: "&nel mundo non bjue mugier que tanto trabajo / njn tanto enojo sofriese / como yo sofry tres dias ha . . . " [fol. 81b]. In short order Miles will burn the hermitage with the holy man inside it, the flames reminiscent of the metaphorical hellfire through which Florençia must pass. The story proceeds to the scene in which Florençia is savagely beaten by the raving sadist and then hung by her hair from a tree and left for dead. The text reads: "& erguyose & fuela tomar por los cabellos./ & puso la ençima de vn arbol / & colgola por ellos" [fol. 82b]. Several times the text repeats this fact: "En tal guisa estaua colgada del aruol / que non llegauan ssus pies a tierra . . . " [fol. 82c]. When Florençia is saved by the chance appearance of a group of hunters in the woods, she is taken back to the castle of Terryn, the leader of the group, and her first *huesped*. He tells his wife, Anglentina, "yendo asy corriendo por la montaña fallamos colgada de vn arbol vna mesquina non se sy es condesa o duquesa . . . " [fol. 83b]. No Christian audience can miss the parallel between Florençia's suffering on the tree and Christ's suffering on the tree at Calvary. Florençia, by the way, sees plenty of parallel between her situation and those of several biblical personages whose names she repeats almost as a litany in a prayer of supplication to God to help her the way he had helped them in their moments of need: Daniel, Elijah, David, the Virgin herself, Joseph. She states: "dios que guardastes a daniel delos leones / & helias el profeta leuastes / quando echo a su diçipulo su manto / & que guardastes a dauit / del jayan golias./ Assy

como vuestra madre naçio en nazareht / & que por vuestro manda-
do fue dada a josep / que la guardase / asy me guardat uos deste
traidor falso que non aya en mj parte . . ." [fol. 81d]. This kind of
prayer is typical of the prayers she makes whenever confronted with
travails. She takes special solace in repeating the names of Our
Lord in several of these situations (fols. 82a and 91c). The similarity
of her situation with those of Jesus, the prophets, and the saints is
evident.

Pilgrims, both literally and symbolically, are present throughout
this text. First, the twin brothers, Esmere and Miles, are told of the
coming war in Rome between Garssir and Otas by a pilgrim from
Hungary on his way back from a visit to Rome (fol. 54d). Next,
there is a series of hosts and hostesses that provide hospice for the
wandering Florençia as she goes from one accusation to the next.
There are both good and wicked *huespedes* among them and in this
way the motif of hospice is linked to a new concern of the compilers, that of discernment – how to tell good ones from bad ones.
Peraut and his wife Ssolipsa present a case in point since they represent both the good and the bad. Ssolipsa is a kind, generous *huespeda* (term used at fol. 90c) who opens her heart and home to the
needful Florençia: "& ssolipsa la burgesa / que muy grant piadat
ajua della entremetiose dela seruir a todo su poder.// ca bien sabia
que en malas manos era cayda / Mas penso que en quanto ella pudiese quela guardaria de mal . . . " [fol. 89a]. Peraut, on the other
hand, described as "muy falso & muy cobdicioso" [*ibid.*] connives
with Clarenbaut, the thief, to sell Florençia to Escot, the sailor.
Clarenbaut, the thief, was saved from hanging by the intervention
of Florençia and has falsely pledged to her his allegiance: "& el le
juro quele non falleçeria por auer del mundo / & quela seruiria leal
mente . . . " [fol. 88d]. The text tells us that she made a great mistake in saving him: "Por que non deue njnguno toller el ladron dela
forca pues es culpado / njn destoruar la justiçia./" [fol. 90d]. Florençia had recruited his services with the same promise we have
seen in the mouth of King William when he retrieved his horn from
the young pilgrim to San Gil: "Par mj fe dixo ella nonbre as de
ladron / Agora dexa tu menester & se bueno / & sy me quesieres
seruir tu aueras ende gualardon . . . " [fols. 88c-d]. Indeed, her
words are even reminiscent of the words of Christ when he called
his disciples to be fishers of men. One, of course, must use discernment in determining whom to trust with discipleship and other

charges. That Florençia fails in this specific case should not surprise us, since Christ, too, failed in at least one case, that of Judas. The text actually compares Clarenbaut to Judas: "Nunca el traidor de judas que en gehethsemanja / vendio nuestro señor alos judios fizo mayor traiçion dela que fara çedo clarenbaut / a florençia de Roma . . . " [fol. 89c]. Elsewhere I have shown how the issue of discernment reappears in the tale of Carlos Maynes (Spaccarelli, "Restoring . . .") when Loys and Barroquer argue whether to trust the thief/magician, Griomoart. If in the case of Clarenbaut a mistake has been made – Florençia would have been better off by following the dictum mentioned above – in the case of Griomoart in the *Carlos Maynes* text, it is the liberated thief who brings about the reconciliation scene, one of the culminating moments of the *LH*. The community of readers and hearers, the pilgrim people, must learn to be wary of rash judgment and thereby learn to discern between good and bad *huespedes* and between contrite thieves and the recalcitrant. It is worth remembering in this context that pilgrims were often criminals themselves who were undertaking their journies as penance for real crimes.

Also worth noting in this context is that the sale of Florençia to Escot is accomplished with the expectation on Florençia's part that she will be undertaking a pilgrimage to the Holy Land. She believes that Peraut and Clarenbaut are arranging passage for her on a ship that is going to take a group "en Romeria al santo sepulcro" [fol. 89d]. Moments earlier she has thought how much she would love to make such a sojourn: "& penso que de grado yria ala tierra ssanta de iherusalem do dios priso muerte / & vida / sy ouiese quien la ayudase & la guiase . . . " [fol. 89c]. Finally, at the end of the tale, kind and loyal *huespedes* are rewarded as per the custom set in earlier texts of the compilation: "A terrin dieron plazençia con todo el Reyno por quanto bien fizo a florençia./" [fol. 99b].

The *Otas* text is special in that it recapitulates not only the life of Christ and the saints in Florençia's suffering, but also because it depicts her as a saint in embryo herself. We see in the circumstances of her life the way in which a saint emerges from the travails of the world with its deception and greed, and we witness the strength faith has in protecting the innocent and in providing miracle-working power. Once the fame of her healings spreads throughout the lands, people of all positions flock to the monastery of Bel Repaire to seek healing from this blessed, but secular, and clearly carnal woman (González rightly insists on this point, "Otas . . ." 188). The spot becomes a site of pilgrimage. Florençia, then, is the perfect middle link in the various levels of recapitulation of the life of Christ: she is like the saints of old (again, Nichols' *in illo tempore*) but is also very much like the medieval readers and hearers who are accordingly learning to see themselves in this eternal trajectory of disciples of Christ.

As mentioned before, there are several themes and motifs that make their initial appearance in the *Otas* text. First, it should be noted that the *Otas* presents a case of male twins who are of noble lineage, thus repeating the motif we have seen in both the *Plaçidas* and the *Gujllelme* texts, but in the case of this new pair of twins (Esmere and Miles/Millon), we have a situation in which one of the pair is an evil counterpoint or foil to his brother. The presentation of the twins insists on their beauty, a new feature in the *LH*, which up to this point had concentrated solely on the beauty of the female protagonists, (even those saints who will undergo a transformation towards ugliness start out with great beauty – see the analysis of Mary the Egyptian, chapter IV.B). Depicting male beauty is typical of courtly romance, yet in the *LH* the handsome males must be distinguished between those whose beauty is a true reflection of their character and those whose beauty hides the ugly truth of sinfulness and depravity (as we have seen above in the discussion of Miles). Furthermore, in these cases male beauty serves to connect the evil male characters to the corporeality usually consigned to females as the heirs to EVE, her origin in the flesh of Adam, and her original sin (see Bloch, "Misogyny" and Robertson, "Corporeality"). The Miles/Esmere split, then, presents the readers and hearers of the *LH* with another episode in which the issue of discernment is brought to the fore.

Another theme or motif that appears for the first time in this section of the *LH* in full development is the matter of magic. Audegons, one of Florençia's ladies in waiting, is shown to make predictions according to horoscopes. Her advice is followed by the upstanding Florençia whose future will turn out to be so saint-like. One is to conclude that magic is both useful and good. The case in point deals with Florençia's worries as to the death of her father and her desire to take a husband who would be a worthy successor to Otas. Audegons tells her:

> Señora dixo audegons yo oue echadas mjs suertes sobre vuestro casamiento / segundo el curso dela luna & delas estrellas / & falle que con vno destos [either Esmere or Miles] aujades de ser./ casada non se con qual dellos./ Bien sabemos que son fijos de grant Rey / & desta guerra ellos leuaron ende mejor prez / mas bien vos digo que esmere es mas fermoso / & de mayor proeza mas cortes./ verdat es dixo florençia./ mas dixieron me / que el otro dia quando mataron a mj padre / que llagaron a el de muerte./ señora diz audegons / vos tomad el mayor / ca mucho es buen cauallero . . . [fols. 67a-b]

The horoscope is correct as far as it goes: one of the twins will indeed be the best choice for a husband. Note that magic too requires the utilization of discernment in determining a proper choice.

The next case of magic has to do with the powerful stone that Florençia utilizes to aid in her healings and to protect her virginity. In tandem with the power of the Lord, the stone is able to inhibit Miles from achieving sexual arousal thereby preserving Florencia's virginity during the sadistic scene in the woods. He accuses her of using "carautulas & melezinas" at this point, a typical attack on his part – projecting his own blackness out onto others. The episode reads as follows:

> & nuestro señor mostro y su virtud / & otrossy le valio y mucho / vna piedra preçiosa que traya enla broncha / entrelas otras / que y eran engastonadas / que auja tal virtud / que mientra la touiese / en njnguna guisa / non / poderia perder su virginidat / Agora oyd como fizo la piedra su virtud / por la misericordia de dios / que do miles cuydo fazer della su voluntad./ perdio todo el poder del cuerpo / & delos nienbros / & ssentiose asy tollido enel canpo / % & despues que ouo poder dessy / & de fablar./ llamo a florençia & dixole. // Puta como sodes encantador / caratulas me auedes fechas / esto non sse puede encobrir./ Mas para aquel señor que el mundo fizo / sy las non desfezierdes / yo uos tajare la cabeça./ Traidor diz florençia dizes muy grant mentira:/ mas la virtud de dios me guardo dety / çertas diz millon de follia pensades / todas vuestras carautulas & vuestras melezinas / cuydo yo toller . . . [fol. 82a]

The readers and hearers of the *LH* know that Florençia's use of this stone is not inappropriate nor is it close to black magic since the stone was a gift to her from her stepfather, the *apostoligo* or Pope. Earlier in the tale she is described in the following way:

> & en ssu cabeçon vna brocha de oro con muy Ricas piedras
> preçiosas enella que auja tal virtud / que non auia enel mundo
> dolor / do con ella tañjesen que sse luego non quitase & otra
> auja y que non ha donzella quela troxiese que pudiese perder ssu
> virginidat:/ mucho daua la piedra grant castidat / & el apostoligo
> la diera a florençia . . . [fol. 79b]

Note that magic here is seen as a gift of God, not as the sinister activity suggested in Miles' accusation. This episode, then, is a fuller treatment of a theme that had its first appearance in the *Cataljna* text where the enraged emperor Maxentius "el brauo enperador" [fol. 21c] accuses his wife, newly converted to Christianity, of having been deceived by enchantment: "engañote ya algunt xristiano por encantamento" *(ibid.)*. He later acuses Cataljna of having perpetrated *encantamento* [fol. 22c]. Note that the issue of discernment is absent in the *Cataljna* text since the various miracles and other activities associated with the saint are without question of divine origin. The two remaining tales in the *LH* will repeat this more developed utilization of magic and thereby repeat the lesson the book makes concerning discernment – the individual must learn to differentiate between good and bad examples in many categories (see Spaccarelli, "Recovering," and below). In *Magic in the Middle Ages*, Richard Kieckhefer makes a distinction between natural and demonic magic. He states:

> . . . medieval Europe recognized two forms of magic: natural
> and demonic. Natural magic was not distinct from science, but
> rather a branch of science. It was the science that dealt with "oc-
> cult virtues" (or hidden powers) within nature. Demonic magic
> was not distinct from religion, but rather a perversion of religion.
> It was religion that turned away from God and toward demons
> for their help in human affairs. (9)

It would seem that readers of the *LH* are asked to make the same distinction as the one described here as typical of that time. One must imagine the pilgrim readers and hearers as individuals determined to experience the presence of divinity in this world. They do this in various ways: by reenacting the Emmaus story in their pilgrimage and thereby embodying guest/host theology; by trekking in search of relics and other physical signs of divine power at shrines and churches all along the pilgrim way; by taking solace and encouragement in the stories of these inspired and blessed individuals who preceded them in the never-ceasing recapitulation of the story of Jesus and his saints; and by being ready to view God's hand at work in situations (such as magic) where the lesser trained or the miscreants would place the devil. [17]

G. De Vna Santa Enperatris

The tale of the *Santa enperatris* is fascinating in many respects. The first comment one must make about it is that it tells an often intimate story without giving specific names to its characters. The individuals in the tale are always denoted by generic determinants such as "la enperatris," "el enperador," "el prinçipe," "los villa-

---

[17] Speaking of God's hand reminds one of the image of God's hand stopping Abraham as he is about to sacrifice Isaac depicted on the typanum of the Puerta del Cordero of Leon's Colegiata de San Isidoro. The pilgrim readers and hearers of the *LH* would surely have stored that image in their mind's eye as they contemplated the power of God and the way it worked in the book they were "reading" and in the experiences they were having as a pilgrim people. Ana Suárez González assures us that pilgrims did indeed pass by the colegiata:

> La llegada frecuente de peregrinos a San Isidoro puede explicarse por varios motivos. San Isidoro se halla en una ciudad, León, de gran importancia en la Ruta Jacobea pero además, desde 1168, el cenobio era paso obligado dentro de la ciudad para todos aquellos que recorrían el Camino Francés ya que en ese año Fernando II decreta el desvío del mismo para hacerlo pasar por delante del templo isidoriano. (56)

One is also reminded of the comments of Hermann Knust of over a century ago in his introductory remarks to his editions of two of the tales included in the *LH*. Our general knowledge of the Middle Ages and our analysis of this specific book argue against his vision of a simple period with a non-complex, even absurd intelectual production. Nevertheless, in the context of speaking of the hand of God, it is worth reproducing his words from *Dos obras didácticas y dos leyendas*:

> Otras eran, como ya dijimos, las miras de la edad media á la cual el sentimiento místico-teológico imprimió su carácter, sirviendo las galas de la poesía para cultivarlo y embellecerlo. Y, en verdad, hacia falta, porque en los primeros siglos de aquella época era tal la ignorancia, que no se podian comprender las ideas abstractas, ni concebir los preceptos de la moral, sino que gustaba ver lo uno y lo otro ilustrado por sencillos cuentos. En todos éstos, importantísimos para los que quieran conocer las aspiraciones de nuestros antepasados, se desarrolla la idea mística de que la mano omnipotente de Dios interrumpe á cada momento el curso ordinario de los acontecimientos, de modo que los hechos más maravillosos y ménos esperados no tienen nada de extraordinario. Si no perdemos esto de vista no extrañaremos lo que se refiere en nuestras historias . . . (87-88)

nos," etc. One is tempted, therefore, to see this tale as unimportant or, worse, as intrinsically flawed. However, in the context of the book for which it was translated, this "generic" story has an extremely important place and an intense attraction. Let us look at some of its details and just how it fits in the structure of the *LH*.

The plot line of the tale follows very closely the story of Florençia in the *Otas*. The empress is falsely accused by her brother-in-law as Florençia was accused by Miles. The accusation is cast in the bitter language of misogyny as has been noted above (see pp. 63-65). As in the *Otas*, the accusation comes as a result of the brother-in-law's having been rejected in love. It is worth noting that the text underscores the brother-in-law's beauty, and consequently his role as a tempter (the role usually assigned to the daughters of Eve), and then the progressive stages of courtly love sickness that he goes through as a result of being rejected by the *enperatris*:

> . . . ssy ante auia alegria torno tan triste / & tan coitado que non sopo que feziese njn que dixiese / asi que dormiendo velaua & velando ssoñaua la mentira tenja por verdat / & la verdat por mentira / Non auia cosa enel mundo de que sabor ouiese / njn podia yr njn venjr / njn se leuantaua del lecho. desi perdio el comer & el beuer & torno magro & feo & amarillo ca mucho auia grant mal./ [fol. 102c]

The *Santa enperatris* reveals the ridiculous and sinful nature of courtly love while indicating it as a phenomenon whose practitioners are males. In this it stands apart from most profeminist works which have been linked to courtly love and its idealization of women (Gerli, *Arcipreste* 38-39). This section of the *LH* (along with the Miles/Florençia episodes in the *Otas*) could easily carry as its subtitle "reprobación del amor mundano." In this sense it is not inappropriate to consider the *LH* a companion text to the *Corbacho* of Alfonso Martínez de Toledo since it coincides with it in "demostrando . . . cómo el amor mundano, a pesar de existir bajo una cobertura de refinamiento y respetabilidad, no es sino pecado y perdición" (Gerli, *Arcipreste* 42).

The lovesickness described above is a direct result of the work of the devil and the "mal amor" he sows in the young man:

> Por aquel donzel que tanto era fermoso/ venja el diablo con sus tentaçiones & con ssus antojamjentos tentar la buena dueña

> mucho era fermoso el donzel & bien fecho / & de muy alto
> linage / mas tanto lo fezo el diablo follon & asi lo abraso &
> ençendio / que le fizo amar de mal amor la mugier de su her-
> mano & de ssu señor / [fols. 100d-101a]

In this case, the emperor, who has been away on a pilgrimage,
believes the false accusation, lashes out against the woman, and sen-
tences her to a horrible and violent death:

> Mas quando la mesquina lo quiso besar / el enperador que venia
> todo tollido de saña & de mal talante [because of the false accu-
> sation]./ ferio la tan toste en medio del Rostro de tan./ grant feri-
> da que dio conella del palafren en tierra muy desonrrada mente
> & non la quiso catar mas / llamo dos de sus sieruos a grandes
> bozes / & dixoles tomad esta aleuosa & echatle vna soga ala gar-
> ganta / & leuadla Rastrando aquel monte / al mas esquiuo logar
> que y vierdes / & y la desmenbrat toda./ [fols. 105c-d]

The role of the enperador is minimal – just enough to show him as
the gullible, unjust brute that he is.

The empress is almost killed by the emperor's henchmen, but
"vn muy alto prinçipe / caualgaua por aquel monte que venja de
aquella Romeria do fuera el enperador" [fol. 106c] comes upon the
scene with his companions and they kill the henchmen, thereby saving the empress. She is taken in by the prinçipe and his wife and
subsequently becomes the nurse to their child. This is a repetition
of the episode in the *Otas* in which Florençia becomes the nurse to
Beatriz, the child of Terrin and his wife, Anglentina. In the Florençia tale, Macayre, a retainer of Terrin, falls in love with the beautiful newcomer, but becomes embittered and mad when rejected.
He consequently kills the child under her tutelage and then plants
the bloody weapon in the hand of the sleeping Florencia, thus trig-
gering another episode of rejection and exile. The exact situation
also occurs in *De vna santa enperatris* when the prinçipe's brother
comes to love the empress, and when rejected, decides to kill the
child and plant the weapon in her hand. The empress is consequently exiled again – this time to a desert island.

In all these episodes the empress is able to see that her sufferings are not in vain: "& partiase vn poco de su pesar / por que bien
veya / que nuestro señor queria ssu alma esaminar / & fazer morrer
en proveza / por la fazer despues floreçer / ca ella bien sabia ver-

dadera mente que nuestro señor ihesu xpisto veno en tierra como pobre de su grado sofrir muerte por los pecadores esto era ssu conforte./." [fols. 107b-c]. This is probably the clearest rendition of the *imitatio Christi* that we have traced throughout the tales of the *LH*. Note that the *imitatio Christi* is again linked to a female protagonist. The reader/hearer is reminded that just as the suffering of the empress recapitulates the suffering of Christ, so too do their hardships recapitulate hers. In fact, the empress is depicted as a pilgrim, not symbolically but literally, and the hardships she undergoes while walking could be easily recognized by any pilgrim:

> & asi ando en muchas Romerias / visitando ssantos & santas./ de guisa que todos ssus paños fueron rrotos / & vsados & ssy su marido feziera su Romeria de cauallo non fue ella ssynon de pie & desque ando por muchas tierras estrañas / & por montes & por valles / & por villas & por castillos / & acabo muchas buenas Romerias llego a Roma / [fol. 117d]

The earlier reference to *proveza* "poverty" is picked up just a few folios later in an interchange with the prinçipe's brother. He has told the empress that as a poor "villana coujgera" [fol. 109a] she has no right to reject him. She replies:

> ssy so pobre non deuo por eso mj alma despreçiar / mas que faria vna señor de vn enperio ca los pobres tanto deuen amar sus almas & tanto sse deuen trabajar delas saluar bien como los Reys & las Reynas / Ca non desama dios alas pobres gentes njn los huerfanos njn las huerfanas ante han tan gran derecho enel rregno delos çielos bien como los Reys & las Reynas / Mas tanto sse paga dios dellos / que por pobreza / non desama njnguno / & ssemejame que non es pobre / njn mendigo ssynon aquel que mal busca / & que mal faz / & aquel es pobre / el que dios desama / ca non val cosa / njn sabe nada . . . [fols. 109a-b]

Here the text shows the egalitarianism we have been tracing throughout the *LH* and in particular ties it to the process of *imitatio Christi*. Also, this relatively detailed discussion of the poor and their rights to the *regno* links this section of the text both in terms of content and vocabulary to those earlier references to the poor that we outlined in the stories of Sts. Mary and Martha (see above, chapter IV.A). The compilers of the *LH* are not content to leave the

matter there however. Just a few folios later the empress is lament-
ing her disgrace in an apostrophe to Fortune and her wheel. Here
the compilers make specific reference to earlier texts in the *LH* and
in so doing they underscore its unity:

> Ay ventura / quanta moujste ensalçada / & como me derribaste
> ende / & me fazes lo peor que tu puedes / ca en mas peligroso
> logar njn mas amargo non me poderias tu echar deste en que yo
> esto Tanto falle en ty de contrario / que mas de mala ventura me
> das me semeja que a todos aquellos que enel mundo fueron /
> Tanto he de desconforto / que me non puedes tu ende dar mas /
> njn as poder de me peor fazer delo que fazes./ Nunca job nin
> *ssant estaçio* / tanto perdieron como yo perdi Ca yo perdi la tie-
> rra & el auer / de mas el cuerpo / mas poco daria por el auer / ssi
> pudiese en tierra auer vn pequeño lugar en que seruiese a dios. /
> [fols. 112d-113a–my emphasis]

Earlier references to magic in the *LH* are likewise repeated in
this story of the santa enperatris. Just as Florençia in the *Otas* was
given the power to heal lepers and to protect her virginity through
use of a magic stone, so too is the empress given the power to cure
by the Virgin herself ("el santo lirio & la rosa que bien huele" [fol.
113b]). The empress, at the very bottom of Fortune's wheel, is comforted by the Virgin in a vision in which she is told that the men
who have abused her and caused all this anguish will be punished:

> & seran descobiertas & contadas las traiçiones & las falsedades
> que te a grant tuerto fezieron & sabe que aquellos que telo bus-
> caron que todos sson gafos podridos. &ntonçe le deuiso como
> feziese / & por que tu non cuydes que esto que ves que es an-
> teparança./ tanto que despertares toda seras confortada de tu
> fanbre./ & aueras alegria & plazer de que me viste / Agora te
> auonda asi de la vista de mj faz que fanbre nonte faga mal./ &
> por que sepas mejor que me viste / tanto que despertares / cata
> so tu cabeça / & fallaras vna santa yerua a que yo dare tal virtud
> / & tal graçia que a todos los gafos / & quien la dieres a beuer
> enel nonbre dela madre del Rey de gloria / que luego seran gua-
> ridos / & sanos / ya tan perdidos non / seran:/. [fol. 114b]

In fact, the empress will make use of this "santa yerua" to cure the
very wretches who caused her so much suffering – another close

parallel to the *Otas* tale. [18] Again, magic is portrayed as "natural" and as a holy gift from above.

In the *Santa enperatris* tale the empress cures the wretched lepers in a scene that brings together the various characters of the story, including the emperor, her husband. Cristina González has discussed this tale and its ending comparing it unfavorably to the *Otas* text ("*Vna santa*" 164-165). González prefers the more worldly and carnal Florençia to the empress, who in a noteworthy rendition of the theme of *contemptus mundi* rejects her husband at the end of the tale and insists on entering holy orders in order to be the bride of Christ:

> Ca quando todo el mundo me echo & me falleçio & me fizo mal &ntonçe me acorrio el piadoso dios & me libro de todos mjs enemigos mortales / & por ende mety / enel asy mi corasçon que es conel soldado & junto / que nunca ende sera desapreso nin partido / por enperador terenal & tan mucho lo amo & tanto me / fio enel / que por todo otro amor do muy poco/ & por ser mas su amigo / los çiclatones & los paños de seda / & los xametes / & los anjllos de oro & todo otro buen guarnjmento / & los buenos comeres & los buenos beueres & todo lo otro viçio por el dexe & dexo / la onrra & la corona del enperio / por ser monja pobre / & quiero ser esposa del Rey delos çielos & pesame que non oue fecho / quando fuy donzella / lo que agora fago . . . [fols. 122b-c]

She rejects earthly, carnal love of the man who betrayed her and who battered her with such violence and with so little reason in order to dedicate herself to "good love":

---

[18] The two females, in their use of stones and herbs of holy origin, seem to be a combination of the "beata," or "holy healers" "so essential to healing work . . . following the tradition of saints such as Santa Monica" (25) and of the "wise woman or empiric," a type "noted especially for . . . knowledge of the healing properties of herbs" (26) described by Mary Elizabeth Perry in *Gender and Disorder in Early Modern Seville*. The *LH* defends women who participate in these healing roles that were consistently seen as verging on the illicit and the diabolical throughout the Middle Ages and the early modern period (see Perry 28-32) by explicitly addressing accusations of diabolical powers in the Florençia/Miles episodes. Perry's study is a sad confirmation that the social vision defended in the *LH* was ultimately unsuccessful and, indeed, suppressed as women healers saw "their value unrecognized" in a hierarchical social system that "relegated the women below, according to perceptions of their power, into the categories of sorcerer or saint" (32).

> . . . mas en amar a dios ssin dubda / non y ha auentura njn caida.
> mas quien lo mas ama & quien lo mejor sierue./ tanto mas
> amado es del / & mejor gualardon ende prende & quien lo mas
> ama / mejor lo ha./ Pues buen señor buen amar faz aquel./ en
> quien *buen amor* non puede pereçer / Ca dios es tan largo que
> non puede enel falleçer ninguno . . . [fol. 122a–my emphasis]

There is no doubt, González is right, the earthy Florençia, with
her attachments to the world and to the flesh, seems both more real
and more satisfactory as a protagonist worthy of our admiration.
However, in the plan of the *LH* this rejection of the abusive,
gullible, unreasonable, wrathful king at the end of a tale that recapitulates so many of the book's key themes will have importance as
we turn to the culminating chapter, the tale of Carlos Maynes and
his wife, Seuilla.

H. THE TALE OF CARLOS MAYNES AND SEUILLA: CLIMAX AND RETURN

In a series of articles, one with John Maier, I have endeavored to
show in what ways the tale of Carlos Maynes and Seuilla is the culminating story of the *LH*. We have used a variety of arguments
ranging from a distinctive feature matrix (Maier/Spaccarelli 21), to
a straight forward Jungian analysis ("Symbolic"), to a reconstruction of the four-folio lacuna in the text in order to demonstrate its
privileged position in the compilation ("Recovering"). Consideration of issues dealing with pilgrimage will confirm these earlier
conclusions and show even more clearly the structural principles
used in compiling the *LH* while underscoring the unity of the book.
Many of the features of the earlier tales are present in the *Carlos
Maynes* text. Queen Seuilla is caught in a compromising situation
that is not of her making (a dwarf has surreptitiously entered her
bed), and she is sentenced first to death at the stake, and then, out
of leniency, she is sent into exile – a symbolic pilgrimage. The sentence proceeds from her husband, the emperor Carlos Maynes, depicted at this early stage of the story as "a rather gullible, indecisive
rationalist" (Spaccarelli, "Symbolic" 5). I assume the medieval read-
er/hearer would be immediately outraged at this injustice both
because of the summary way in which Carlos dispenses "justice"

without even questioning his wife, [19] and because they have been conditioned by earlier episodes of the *LH* to see kings in a negative light (one thinks immediately of the violent emperor in *De vna santa enperatris,* see also p. 91 above).

Seuilla is expelled from the court and wanders through the *floresta* with the aid of a series of guides of various social ranks (Aubery de Mondisder; Barroquer, the *villano*; the Apostoligo or Pope of Rome; her uncle, the warrior/hermit) who protect her from the villains who inevitably seek to take her sexually. The queen and her guides, particularly the early episodes with Barroquer, provide an image comparable to the Holy Family's flight into Egypt (one must remember that Seuilla is pregnant at this time) and therefore reminiscent of earlier episodes of the *LH* (the tale of Plaçidas and his wife Teospita and the King William story). Of course, "flight into Egypt" is also an image of pilgrimage. The queen says to Barroquer upon meeting him: "& començe de fuyr quanto pude / & non sse para do vaya./ & sso muy coitada/. ca ando preñada./ & por dios ome bueno / consejad me oy / si uos plaz . . ." [fol. 130b]. Barroquer responds: "dueña non temades / Ca para aquel dios que naçio en betlem / dela virgen santa maria / por su plazer que ya non yredes sin / mj vna legua de tierra que yo non vaya convusco . . ." [fol. 130c]. A few lines later he tells her: ". . . & a uos converna de yr por estrañas tierras / fasta que seades libre dela criatura / que en vos traedes . . ." [fol. 130d]. Note the convergence of many of the key words indicative of the "Gregorian pattern" and the proximity of the reference to Bethlehem and the Virgin birth which serve to remind the readers and hearers that in these travails Seuilla is experiencing the *imitatio Christi.*

This image of fleeing through the wilderness is repeated later in the text when Seuilla, Barroquer, and her son Loys decide to take leave of Urmesa where they have resided for over ten years in the home of certain generous hosts:

> &ntonçe troxieron ala dueña vna muleta./ & el donzel se fue al Rey / & espediose del./ desy tornose & fuese con su madre / & barroquer yua delante ssu sonbrero enla cabeça. & ssu bordon grande & bien ferrado fiera mente/. Mucho era grande el villano a desmesura / & mucho arreziado / & de como era grande / &

---

[19] See Spaccarelli, "Symbolic," 5-7 for more details concerning this situation.

fuerte / & feo loys quelo cato tomose a Reyr: / desta guisa en-
traron en su camjno, & andaron tanto fasta que llegaron a vn
monte / que auja siete leguas de ancho / & otro tanto de luengo
/ do non auja villa njn poblado / mas de vna hermita mucho
metida enel monte. &nel monte andauan doze ladrones que
fazian grant mal / & grant muerte enlos que pasauan / por el
camjno / & barroquer que vio el monte verde & las aues cantar
por los Ramos a grant sabor de ssy / por sabor del buen tienpo /
& por alegrar a su señora / començo de yr cantando / a muy
grant voz asi quel monte ende Reteñja muy lueñe./ [fols. 140c-d]

Note that the typical accoutrements of a pilgrim are attributed to
Barroquer in this scene in which he portrays a kind of singing pilgrim (a possible repetition of the scene in the tale of Mary the
Egyptian in which Zozimas is portrayed in a similar light, see above,
chapter IV.B). This portion of text mentions the ugliness and huge
size of Barroquer, a recurring motif both in *Carlos Maynes* and in
the *LH* in general (see above, chapter IV.B). The ugliness of Barroquer has been studied by myself ("Symbolic" 8 and note 27) and by
John R. Maier ("Of Accused Queens"). Both point out the physical
similarities between him and the dwarf, and Maier speaks of connections with "the folkloric theme of beauty and the beast" (27).
The *LH* portrays Barroquer as a *villano* whose actions are consistently noble and altruistic (see above, pp. 77-78). The readers and
hearers of the *LH*, who might otherwise jump to a conclusion following the commonplace "relationship between ugliness and un-
favorable traits" (Maier "Of Accused Queens" 28), are reminded
again that one must use discernment in ascertaining the true nature
of any given character or situation. The importance of such discernment is evident when one considers the *LH* as a whole in which so
many characters are ugly. Mary the Egyptian is one whose ugliness
emerges as her spiritual stock is enhanced. On the other hand, the
various lepers of both the *Otas* and *Santa enperatris* tales take on
what seem to be exterior signs of their inner repugnance and sin.
Barroquer and the dwarf are characters whose ugliness is inherent
to them from birth and not dependent on any moral, ethical or religious issues. This variety of ugly characters in the *LH* confirms Harriet Goldberg's assertion in her survey of ugliness in Castilian literature that "there was no one stereotypically ugly woman nor was
there a typically ugly man . . ." ("Several Faces" 88). Suffice it to say

that in stressing Barroquer's ugliness the text repeats a motif that it first included in the tale of St. Mary Egyptian, some 120 folios earlier. The world depicted in the *LH* is one whose signs must be deciphered with great care.

In their pilgrimage through "*tierras estrañas*" Seuilla and Barroquer are given hospice by a series of commoner *huespedes* whose noble and "courtly" acts of generosity are rewarded handsomely at the end of the tale. The first of these *huespedes* is a *burges* who responds positively to Barroquer's request for aid:

> & el burges Respondio & dixo ala dueña./ Amiga yo non se quien vos sodes njn de qual linage. mas he deuos grant piadat en mj corasçon./ & por ende aueredes la posada a vuestra voluntad / que vos non costara vna meaja./ quando barroquer esto oyo / gradeçiogelo mucho./ & entonçe deçendieron / & el huesped que era sabidor & cortes. / guysoles muy bien de comer / & deque comjeron quanto quesieron / . . . . [fol. 131b]

The next set of *huespedes* will be in the city of Urmesa, Hungary which is where Queen Seuilla gives birth to her son Loys. The hosts, Joserant and his wife, are described as follows: "& posaron en casa de vn Rico burges / que auja su mugier muy buena & de buena vida que fezieron muy bien serujr la Reyña / . . ." [fols. 138c-d]. Their attitude towards their guests is one of limitless generosity. When the empress, Barroquer, and Loys are ready to depart to Constantinople after a sojourn of more than ten years (the empress had taken ill) we are told:

> Entonçe fezieron saber al huespet / & ala huespeda que sse querian yr / & la huespeda le dixo./ dueña vedes aqui vuestro fijo / que es fermoso & bueno / çertas que yo lo Amo mucho / que es mj afijado / & bien cuydo / & asy melo diz el corasçon / que avn dende me verna bien:/ Pues que asi es / que uos yr queredes./ tomad de mjs djneros / quantos menester ayades./ dueña dixo barroquer./ grandes merçedes ssy yo bjuo luenga mente./ quanto bien vos feziestes / todo vos sera bien gualardonado / sy dios quesier./ [fol. 140c]

In addition to *huespedes* proper, there is a series of helpmates to the queen and her son who parallel characters or situations that obtained earlier in the *LH*. Griomoart, the thief/magician is the most important of these characters. His first appearance is among a gang of outlaws who set upon the wayfaring Seuilla, Loys, and, Barroquer. Loys and Barroquer fight the men off, killing all of them except for one, Griomoart, who requests clemency in exchange for a treasure that he promises to deliver to Loys: "& sy me dexardes beujr grant pro vos ende verna / & dezir vos he como. Non ha enel mundo thesoro tan ascondido / njn tan guardado / en torre njn en çillero / que uos lo yo non de todo . . . " [fol. 141b]. This is a repetition of the motif of *thesoro* which was used earlier in the *LH* in the tale of Mary the Egyptian (see above, chapter III.B, p. 57). Barroquer, ever the skeptic, warns Loys against such clemency in words that are reminiscent of the dictum presented in the *Otas* in a similar situation (see above, pp. 84-85). Barroquer states: "buen fijo diz barroquer / nunca te fies en ladron / ca aquel quelo quita dela forca a ese furta el mas toste / & ese sse falla del peor . . . " [fols. 141b-c]. As discussed earlier, Florençia in the *Otas* made a mistake in freeing a criminal. Here, in the *Carlos Maynes*, Loys responds to his stepfather Barroquer with the following words: "Non dixo loys / mas veamos / lo que nos dende verna./ mas avn creo que nos Ayudemos del si lo bien quesier fazer / . . ." [*ibid.*]. As I have pointed out in "Recovering . . . ," Loys is shown to have been the wiser in this decision. "He has had the ability to perceive Griomoart's true nature and at this point in the tale this discernment is recognized as one of the attributes of the rightful heir to the kingdom" (222). The text makes plain that Griomoart's activities, which involve liberal use of a magic powder,[20] are fundamental to the family reconciliation that takes place near the end of the tale (See Spaccarelli "Symbolic" and "Restoring" for more details concerning Griomoart, the *thesoro* he promises, his magic, and his important role in the tale). To state matters in another way, we have a commoner helpmate, whose life is spared through application of proper discernment, and whose main activity involves magic – all fundamental themes and elements that we have observed in earlier portions of the book.

We should not be surprised, then, to discover that these commoner guides, *huespedes,* and helpmates are all rewarded well at the

---

[20] Griomoart's magic and his use of a special powder to "heal" the royal family are a transgendered repetition of earlier healings in the *LH*. In the *Otas* text Florençia healed by means of a magic stone. Later the santa enperatris did so by means of a holy herb. In the *Carlos Maynes* text Griomoart's activities lead to the healing of a family instead of individuals.

end of the tale. They are given titles, appointments, and their children are married properly by the emperor. Barroquer is presented formally in court by his stepson Loys:

> Aquel dia tomo loys a barroquer por la mano / & fuelo enpresentar ante el enperador su padre / Señor yo vos do este ome./ por tal pleito / que uos le dedes en vuestra casa tal cosa que uos gradeçamos / ca mucho nos serujo bien en estrañas tierras / que asy bien meresçia por ende ducado / o condado por tierra./ [fol. 151b]

The emperor responds: "Buen fijo dixo el Rey / yo fare lo que uos quesierdes .dole el mayordomadgo de mj corte / & el castiello de menleut por heredat / . . . " [*ibid*.]. And the emperor Ricardo of Constantinople dubs him a knight. Griomoart is made the "copero mayor" [fol. 151c] of the young prince Loys, and the *huesped* of Urmesa, Joserant, is made the emperor's "repostero" and given a yearly stipend [fol. 152a].

These noble acts and rewards contrast sharply with the villainous, violent, and dastardly acts and attitudes of many members of the upper class and of the kings and emperors. The major villain of the *Carlos Maynes* is a certain Macaire, a member of the treacherous clan of Galalon, who is described as "macaire el traidor dela dulçe palabra / & delos fechos Amargos . . ." [fol. 126b] (are we not to think of the "lengua polida como fol" [fol. 107b] mentioned above in section III.C?). He is the favorite of Carlos Maynes, which is evidence of the king's lack of discernment and of his gullibility. This fact, by the way, is not lost on many of the other members of Carlos' court, one of whom, don Aymes, talks of the king's favorite in nothing less than scornful terms: "macaire / este vuestro priuado" [fol. 133b]. Macaire has attempted to rape Seuilla in the first stage of her exile; kills her first guide, Aubery de Mondisder; and plots with his clansmen all kinds of sinister ways to thwart the process of justice when it becomes clear that he must fight a judicial duel with Aubery's faithful dog. In fact, they even contemplate the murder of Carlos Maynes himself. In the words of a clansman, Gonbaut de Piedralada: "Amigo macaire / Aquesto es bien sabida cosa / que aquel galgo non podera durar contra uos & desquelo vos matardes aueremos todos grant alegria. & ayuntar nos hemos entonçe todos a desora / & matemos a carlon que tantas viltanças nos ha fechas por toda su tierra" [fol. 136a]. Perhaps even more sinister than this murder conspiracy is the confidence they have that if need be, they will be able to buy the emperor's clemency. In the judicial duel, the emperor has commanded that neither of the combatants receive aid from others, yet Galerans de Belcaire, one of Macaire's relatives, states: "yre acorrer a macaire / ca le matare el galgo / que no ha escarnidos / mas si me el Rey pudier prender / prometedle por mj / mill marcos & muchos paños de seda / :& el tomar los ha de buena mente / :& asi sera macaire acorrido & Redemjr se ha / & el galgo sera muerto / . . ." [fol. 137b]. This clan of traitors is able to maintain its power and status by manipulating the emperor by means of his flaws and weaknesses, in this case his greed and gullibility.

It is also worth noting that if the retinue of *huespedes*, guides, and helpmates is seen to reflect the process of *imitatio Christi*, these upper-class traitors reject such a prospect out of hand and represent instead a shadow world of lust, conspiracy, and sin. In the moments just before the judicial duel, the relics of St. Stephen are brought before the assembled masses in order for the combatants (in this case the combatant, since Macaire is the only human combatant) to pledge themselves to the saint and entreat his approval of their endeavors:

> & el Rey mando enla plaça estender vn tapete / & fizo y poner / la arca de la Relicas de sant esteuan./ Macaire dixo el obispo yd besar aquellas santas Reliquias / & asi seredes mas seguro de vuestro fecho acabar / Señor dixo macaire por buena fe / non y besaria / njn Ruego a dios // que contra vn can me ayude asi dixo el malandante // mas non ouo / ome enel canpo quelo oyese / que se no santiguase / & que non dixiese que malandante fuese & malapreso escontra el galgo / asy como le tenja tuerto./ entonçe fezieron leuar las Reliquias / a la eglesia / pues vieron que macaire non seles quesiera omillar njn llegar se a ellas./ [fol. 136c]

The pilgrim readers and hearers, who are making their way to Compostela to worship before the relics of St. James and who encounter other holy relics all along the way, need no guidance in perceiving the corrupt nature of a character who haughtily flaunts his independence from the spiritual world represented by the coffer containing the relics of St. Stephen. The pilgrim readers and hearers would probably also remember the earlier reference to relic chests in the tale of Mary the Egyptian (see above IV.B, p. 57).

The *Carlos Maynes* tale is also significant in that its characters, particularly queen Seuilla, inhabit a world that is very much like the world of the reader/hearer in the sense that their experience knows of no saint nor of any miracle, characteristics that were so much part of the world depicted in the book's earlier tales. Yet the queen and her troop of companions represent decency and maintain faith every bit as well as the earlier characters of the *LH* who had the benefit of saintly presence, supernatural messages, or miraculous occurrences. Also, in their travails and sufferings and in the way they contrast with the evil henchmen of the piece they carry forward the focus the book has on the process of *imitatio Christi* since their struggles parallel those of the earlier characters. This is an important step in the ideology of the book, since if these "normal" characters can follow in the line of the saints and pious individuals represented up until this tale, then it is only one step further to include the readers and hearers themselves – the real focus of the book. The *Carlos Maynes* tale is crucial, then, in this plan.

This final, culminating tale focuses on the reader/hearer in another way. Of all the pilgrim-like characters presented throughout the book, Barroquer, the protector and guide to Seuilla and Loys, is the clearest and least ambiguous in that his role as pilgrim requires no interpretation or symbolic understanding. Once the retinue of queen Seuilla arrives in France, Barroquer requests permission to visit the wife and family he had abandoned in order to take care of the exiled and suffering queen. He receives permission to undertake the trip and he is described as a *penjtençial* [fol. 143a] and a *palmero* [fol. 143d and *passim*] and wears the garb and carries the accoutrements known to be traditional to pilgrims (esclaujna, bordon, esportilla, etc.): "&ntonçe sse guiso barroquer / aguysa de penjtençial / & tomo vna grant esclaujna / & vna esportilla & bordon enla mano & vn capirote / & ssonbrero grande / que todo el Rostro le cobria . . . " [fol. 143a]. Barroquer has undertaken a journey of discovery and reunion, first outward and into the unknown (with queen Seuilla) and then back to his home town, identified in the manuscript as none other than Emmaus (*emaus* in the text–fol. 143a), lest we miss the parallel, where at first he is unrecognized by his wife and family. He requests hospice: "que dios vos salue./ albertgat me / ca non se para do vaya . . . " [fol. 143b] and is taken in by them, as preparation for the recognition scene (a repetition of what we have seen so often in earlier episodes of the book) that will come shortly after sharing a meal and a test of the wife's chastity.[21] No reader of the *LH* should be surprised to discover that in this part of the text both Barroquer and his wife are designated *huesped* [fol. 143d] and *huespeda* [fol. 143c] respectively. He is, in fact, an archetypical pilgrim following in the tradition of the Emmaus story, a verbal counterpart to the visual image provided by the famous relief in the cloister of the monastery of Santo Domingo de Silos.

Barroquer's importance as a pilgrim character, however, is not limited to these elemental similarities to the Emmaus story. In fact, he serves as an alter ego for the emperor himself:

> When the Greek army arrives in France to fight for Seuilla's rights, Barroquer requests and receives permission from Seuilla to go off to see the wife and family he has not seen in many years. To expedite this journey, he dons the garb of a pilgrim (*palmero*). It is significant that as the alter ego or shadow of Carlos he makes this long journey in the king's stead. Even more significant is that once at home Barroquer decides to test his wife's fidelity, a test that she wins quite easily. The chastity of Barroquer's wife is equal to that of Seuilla, and in this way the text establishes a parallel between the untarnished wife of Barroquer and Seuilla. (Spaccarelli, "Symbolic" 8)

After the reunion with his family the tale takes him back to Seuilla and her retinue by way of Paris, the court of Carlos Maynes. There Barroquer meets the great king and gives him much news of his wife, his son, and the Greek army that threatens to defeat and depose him. Earlier (see above, pp. 77-78) we have discussed how Barroquer is able to steal the emperor's favorite horse at this point while leaving his own pilgrim's cloak in exchange, hence suggesting that the emperor should undertake a pilgrimage similar to the one Barroquer had just finished. There is, however, no mention of such a royal pilgrimage in the text of the *LH*. Yet all pilgrims to Santiago know that Charlemagne is the mythic first pilgrim to Santiago and therefore patron and founder of the pilgrim tradition–a story nar-

---

[21] See my "Symbolic" (8-9) for another perspective on these important scenes.

rated in the other Book of St. James, the *Liber Sancti Jacobi*. According to Walter Starkie:

> The Book of St. James was intended by the propagandists of Cluny to be an account of the great pilgrimage written at the height of its fame, and they created the personality of Archbishop Turpin [the supposed author of the fourth book of the *Liber*], the faithful prelate of Charlemagne in Cluny, with the object of giving wider significance to the cult of the Apostle and of reviving the mystical heroism of Charlemagne and Roland. Charlemagne would thus become the first pilgrim of St. James, and his knights, who in the original *Chanson de Roland* died as martyrs on the return from the Crusade of 778, would now, in Turpin's account, die at Roncevaux on the return from the pilgrimage to Galicia. (40)

In this fourth book of the *Liber* Charlemagne is said to have had a dream of the Milky Way in which St. James appears and explains the meaning of the starry way. Charlemagne is consequently recruited to make pilgrimage and become the benefactor of the Road (Melczer 31-32).

The *LH* offers an alternative to Turpin's account of Charlemagne's motivation for making pilgrimage: Barroquer's suggestion to the great monarch in the exchange episode. Barroquer, the good and just, leaves his pilgrim's *esclaujna* to Carlos, the unjust, rash, gullible, patriarchal monarch, who has been deceived by his *priuados* (the clan of Galalon). He suggests that Carlos must cleanse himself of the mistakes he has made – do penance – in short, become the *penitençial* following his commoner alter ego, Barroquer. The story of *Carlos Maynes* brings the *LH* to a close with a reconciliation among the various family members: Carlos Maynes, Seuilla, Loys, et al. Yet the ending is as weak and unconvincing as the ending of the *Burlador de Sevilla* according to the interpretation of Bruce Wardropper. He describes an "atmosphere of political corruption. . . . While there is nothing wrong with the social order itself, there is something wrong with those who head and administer it. And the error of these men is not political, but ethical. Expediency, disguised as prudence, has replaced moral judgment in them" (64). No wonder he sees the mass wedding at the end of the play, what should normally be interpreted as the symbol of re-established order, as "a grave affair" (71). Just as the audience of the Golden

Age play leaves the theater wondering what kind of order has been restored by the weak, deceived, and deceiving king (see Wardropper 64, and note 7) who has put his trust in a corrupt *privado*, so too do the readers and hearers of the *LH* wonder about this ending of the *Carlos Maynes*. True reconciliation will require more than can be seen here; it will require contrition and penance – a pilgrimage. The medieval reader/hearer knows from "history" that Carlos did indeed do a pilgrimage to Santiago and that he became the protector and patron of the pilgrimage route – a benefactor and patriarch in the best sense. I believe the text comes full circle here. In identifying themselves with Barroquer, their fellow pilgrim, the readers and hearers symbolically join him in urging pilgrimage and reconciliation upon Charlemagne, and consequently they form part of the very foundation of the tradition in which they are participating. In this way the *LH* reinterprets the mythic history of the Road while motivating and validating the pilgrim community that is both its subject matter and its audience.

We have seen that from its very beginning the *LH* makes participation available to its readers and hearers through the various levels of *imitatio Christi* and the ways in which the readers and hearers identify themselves with the characters of the book. Here in the very last tale, that identification centers on the most obvious pilgrim character of all, Barroquer. In that way the reader/hearer fulfills the ideological purposes and structural design of the compilers: the fiction allows them to come full-circle and be at the same time contemporary, flesh and blood pilgrims, and also "participants" in the founding of the tradition. In *Shards of Love*, María Rosa Menocal reminds us that medieval writers "believed there was a conflation of History and Memory and of personal and universal histories . . ." (16). Later she speaks of the need to develop "synchronic reading" (18) in which we drop a paradigm that privileges perspective, diachrony, and progress, and return to one that allows us to relate to a story (and to history) synchronically. Menocal uses the words "radical presentness" to describe this new paradigmatic view. It is exactly the kind of reading I assume pilgrims did as they sought out the presence of the sacred in the here and now of their own lives. Their reward in this endeavor was participation in the very story they were reading. In this participation they augment their self-esteem and self-confidence knowing that they are companions to hosts of saints and holy workers, from Saints Mary and

Martha to Barroquer. One can imagine them becoming forceful advocates for the egalitarian, christological principles of pilgrimage as developed in the *LH* thereby meriting the reward that is depicted so delightfully in the fifteenth-century stained glass *Coronatio Peregrinorum* from Karlsruhe where St. James distributes crowns to his faithful followers. In this sense the *LH* and its community of pilgrims represent well the concept of a textual community as put forth by Brian Stock:

> From textual communities is was a short step to new rituals of everyday life, whether these were imposed by a monastic rule, a lay confraternity, the search for civic equality, or the ethical values arising from literature itself. . . . Heretics, reformers, *pilgrims*, crusaders, proponents of communes, and even university intellectuals began to define the norms of their behavior, to seek meaning and values over time, and to attempt to locate individual experience within larger schemata. ("Medieval Literacy" 18) [my emphasis]

The "larger schemata" in this case is the vision of pilgrims and pilgrimage provided by the *LH*. Stock's idea is expressed in a slightly different way by Horacio Santiago-Otero in the "Discurso de apertura" of a collection of studies concerning monastic hospitality along the pilgrimage route to Santiago:

> De este modo, surgen vínculos que permanecen más allá del final de la peregrinación. Se pasa a formar parte de una nueva "societas" supranacional, separada del territorio de origen, pero ligada a la vida; una "societas", que no tiene reglas escritas, pero sí afinidades, signos de identidad, intereses y necesidades comunes; es como una nueva y compleja sociedad, en la cual el peregino español o el portugués, el italiano o el francés, el inglés, el alemán, el flamenco, el eslavo, y todos los demás, se reconocen; una sociedad de personas, que, siendo de proveniencia, de condición social y de cultura diversas, tienen durante muchos meses o, tal vez, años, una meta y unos problemas comunes . . . , con unas reglas, símbolos y comportamientos transmitidos por la tradición y garantizados por las estructuras peculiares surgidas en torno a la peregrinación, tales como las cofradías y los hospitales. (12)

However, where Santiago-Otero dismisses the idea of "reglas escritas" I would offer the *LH* as an example of a text which bonded and bound the pilgrims to a particular set of concepts and to a certain consciousness given shape in the book they had read (or heard) along the way to Santiago. Thus, when he says that "con los peregrinos viajaban también ideas, instituciones, leyendas; en una palabra, importantes elementos culturales . . ." (13) I would add both "textos" and "ética social" to his list of "elementos culturales."

I. CONCLUSION

Throughout this study of the various tales that make up the *LH* we have seen the importance given to the figure of the pilgrim and the related character constellation of the guest/host. Our analysis shows in which ways the *LH* validates and affirms its pilgrim reader/hearer, and how it incorporates him/her as a participant through the principle of *imitatio christi* and by opening its culminating scenes to reader participation. I cannot claim that this reading is the only approach to the *LH*, however, if the book served as a pilgrim's companion, as I propose above, then we must now allow it to take a preeminent place in the canon of pilgrimage literature. Sadly, one would search in vain for references to the *LH* in the manuals dedicated to pilgrimage literature. One thinks most readily of Chapter II (Parte Tercera) "Las peregrinaciones y la literatura" of the Vázquez de Parga volumes where texts that have little or nothing to do with the pilgrimage route are listed because they have a single reference to Santiago whereas the *LH*, a voluminous book dedicated to the pilgrim community, is excluded since it makes no specific reference to Santiago. One hopes that the present analysis will rectify this distortion.

CHAPTER V

THE MATTER OF TRANSLATION

It has long been known that the *LH* is a translation from a series of Old French originals. It has been the practice to edit the various "works" of the codex collating the Old Spanish with the Old French "source" texts. The source texts have often been used to "correct" the *LH* versions, and have provided the "norm" for discussing (1) the adequacy of the translation processes, (2) the linguistic, cultural, and literary knowledge and ability of the various supposed translators, and (3) the ways in which the Spanish texts amplify, reduce, or change the source texts. Usually it is in this context that editors and critics speculate as to the purposes, aims, and artistic goals of the translators.

I have shown above how the tradition of publishing and studying in isolation the constituent parts of the *LH* has led to the lamentable situation in which the work as a unified whole has remained unrecognized (as late as 1991 it was still being called a "miscelánea" – see Víctor Infantes 168). In this section I propose to look at the tradition of commentary concerning the translation processes in order to ascertain in which ways it too contributes to the fragmentation of the work. A new orientation concerning the matter of translation goes hand in hand with the literary analysis above in establishing the unity of the *LH*.

Roger M. Walker is without doubt the dean of *LH* studies. His editions (*Santa María Egiçiaca, Plaçidas*) and studies (*Otas*) are essential in establishing the importance of h.I.13 in medieval Spanish literature. In addition, he consistently shows a sensitivity to the unity of the collection and respect for the work of a conscious compiler. However, because he usually focuses his work on single texts and on a critical approach that privileges the relationship of source text to the Castilian text being commented upon, he contributes to the ways in which the *LH* has been misread.

In his sound and learned article dealing with the translation of the *Otas* text ("From French Verse"), Walker proves beyond much doubt that the Spanish translation was based on a lost French prose version and not on the extant *Chanson de Florence de Rome*. Since "the compiler of MS h.I.13 was a simple translator" (237) the innovations to be found in the *Otas* text must have been the work of the Old French prosifier. According to Walker, "his [the prosifier's] main technique is to prune the *Chanson's* luxuriant descriptions, . . . and to impose cuts . . ." (237-238). The *Chanson* could afford such 'luxuries' since it was intended as an entertainment to be sung or recited for an aristocratic audience. Walker envisions a "'theatrical' almost 'operatic'" (240) performance. The prose versions (both the French and the Spanish) were meant for a different audience:

> He is writing for a reading public, for people who are in search of instruction as well as entertainment and who, in Doutrepont's words, 'ne lisent pas volontiers un long poème en vers quand ils ne veulent que connaître l'*histoire*' (p. 394). His appeal is thus much more to the intellect than to the senses and emotions. By rigorously pruning the rhetorical, poetic, and dramatic flights of his model he gains tighter narrative coherence and brings the didactic element of the story into much sharper focus. (240)[1]

Earlier in his article Walker provided examples of where the rich, luxuriant, sensual poetry of the *Chanson* had been stripped to "a matter of fact narrative which preserves the elements essential to the story, and little else" (239). Benaim de Lasry in her edition of the *Santa enperatris* and *Carlos Maynes* arrives at a similar conclusion concerning the two works she is editing: "The Spanish prose romance is of limited length; it has an economical style lacking poetical elaborations" (69). Although she perceives what she calls the "author/translator" in a far more positive light than Walker.

My appreciation for the prose text differs from this assessment. First, I do find the *Otas* text to be relatively rich in description. As

---

[1] See above, chapter IV.B, for a discussion of the divergent ways in which Walker and I conceive of the intended audience of the *LH*.

evidence I would offer the following passages: (1) the "loor de Roma" [fols. 52b-c]; (2) the description of Garssir's battle tent [fol. 54a]; (3) the description of Otas' chariot [fols. 59d-60a]; and (4) the prose version of a "June" song [fol. 68a]. Following Walker and Benaim de Lasry, who work backwards to their sources, one might reply that these examples are probably mere fragments of what the original poetic versions had been. I would claim, however, that the medieval readers did not have before them the French poetic text and were therefore unaware of the paring down of "beautiful passage[s] into matter-of-fact-narrative" (Walker 239). Instead, what they had was their experience of the whole of the *LH*, a text which appeals not only to their intellects, emotions, and senses, but also requires knowledge of the various other texts in the codex, of art and iconography, of history, and of Christo-mimesis–all elements common to pilgrimage, that is, the reader's daily experience. These are also the very structural elements that give coherence and meaning to the *LH*, as we have seen above.

In other words, if one reads the *Otas* text against its "splendid" (Walker 241) source in more or less isolation from the other texts of the *LH*, it is possible to conclude that the Spanish text is more matter of fact, less poetic, "pedestrian" (Walker 241), and aimed at having a didactic impact on an audience more interested in "histoire" than in art. However, if one reads the *Otas* text in the context of the *LH*, one sees it as central to the compilers' goals of building a pilgrim community, of defending women against lascivious males, of inculcating the principles of *imitatio Christi*, and of requiring of its readers the use of discernment concerning beauty and magic. Instead of seeing it as a less perfect text, the product of a diminishing translation and compression process, one sees it as a remarkable text forming part of a complex grid of correspondences that is a unique artistic creation which would have required an equally artistic effort of reading (Dagenais' "*lectio*" and "*electio*" – *Ethics* 8) on the part of its audience.

I have used Walker as an example, since he has worked with h.I.13 more than most scholars, knows the codex well, and has provided a starting point and example for subsequent editors in looking at their texts as isolated translations. I propose we step back for a moment and contemplate the *LH* as a whole. As we have seen above, the nine tales have been put together in an orderly fashion in terms of geographical setting, chronology, and distance from divine presence. They display thematic unity and share a cluster of key words. These facts lead me to believe that the compilers (who are also translators) chose the works they translated and ordered the finished products consciously. If I am right, then it seems appropriate to take their project into account when contemplating any given portion of the text.

To study the tale of *Santa Maria Egiçiaca*, for instance, in terms of the textual history of the tale (see Snow) is a worthy enterprise. It is meaningful to know where in the tradition our specific text falls and how accurate it might be in representing that tradition. Likewise, it is useful to know that any given tale is a saint's life and that it is part of a whole tradition of Christian hagiography (Walsh/Thompson). It is also absolutely essential that one know that at some point in their genesis these texts were translated from poetic versions into prose and that such a process abbreviates the text in specific ways (Walker "From French Verse"). It is also quite interesting to compare the Spanish texts with their sources to ascertain in which ways they have changed what was said in the original.

As an example of this last concern, let us take the study of Rees-Smith concerning the translations of the tales of Saints Mary and Martha where he mentions "numerous mistakes, to be explained mostly by ignorance or inattention . . ." (xxxvi). In fact he tabulates the defects of the Spanish text in terms of (1) defective knowledge of French; . . . (2) those provoked by so-called 'faux amis'; (3) errors of syntax; (4) "misreadings" (xxxvii). He also lists those points at which the Spanish texts improve upon their sources through a series of felicitous additions, omissions, or outright changes. However, by the end of Rees-Smith's exposition one is left with the distinct impression that the translations are the flawed product of inexpert craftsmen. From a very limited data base (the texts of Mary and Martha together make up only 7 folios of the 151+ folios of the codex) Rees-Smith produces a table of statistics (xlvi) concerning the translations which lead him to conclude that the two texts were translated by different persons with "different linguistic habits and different degrees of skill and of knowledge of French" (xlvii). Although Rees-Smith is very aware of the connection between the codex and the Road to Santiago (see xvii) he makes no other speculations or conclusions concerning the translation process.

My proposal is to see the actual act of translation as only one moment in a series of decisions and choices that make up a larger process: the planning and creation of the *LH*. Among these activities would be the selection of texts appropriate for illustrating the themes and issues the compilers had in mind, followed by a conscious choice of key terms and lexical items that would be favored in the text to be produced. I believe I have shown above exactly what those themes and lexical items are, and that they are present consistently from the first folios of the codex to the concluding scenes of the *Carlos Maynes* tale.

If we look at each text and translation in isolation we are very likely to pass over the ingenious and amazingly creative effort made by the compilers to produce their book and we will continue to see the codex as nothing more than a miscellany. This is unacceptable and must be amended if we are to approach this codex and medieval Spanish literature without blinders.

As a counter-balance to the statistical evidence offered by Rees-Smith I would present the following set of facts. Keep in mind that the fragment of the life of Martha is approximately twice the length of the Magdalene fragment as preserved in the *LH*. As we have seen above (chapter IV.A), the Mary Magdalene text presents a case of pilgrimage and, indeed, makes use of the lexical field *romero/romeria* nine times. The life of Martha, a tale which presents the saint as a quintessential hostess, makes use of the lexical field *huesped/huespeda/huespede* seventeen times (approximately twice the number of occurences of *romero/romeria* above). That is to say, the two parts of the story (since I believe the two tales are nothing more than two sides of the same coin), which present in succession the complementary issues of pilgrimage and hospice, are marked by a statistical equivalence or balance in the use of the key lexical items related to their principal themes. In short, statistics can be produced that argue with the same quasi-scientific impact against Rees-Smith's postulation of two distinct translators and in favor of the work's unity.

Once again we are led back to the same set of fascinating questions, considerations, and themes concerning the nature and genesis of the *LH*. In fact, in considering the processes of translation that produced the *LH*, should we not give as much (if not more) attention to the purposes the translators might have had in producing their text as we give to the fidelity they have to their source texts? Most approaches to portions of the *LH* have been to this latter consideration.

In a monumental study of medieval grammar, rhetoric, and translation, Rita Copeland has found it useful to distinguish between two types of translation which she designates primary and secondary. Whereas primary translations serve and supplement a textual authority (the source in our case) acting as an exegesis of the text, secondary translations "give precedence to rhetorical motives, defining themselves as independent productive acts" (177). In addition, she claims that secondary translation "designates, among other things, the building of a native literary tradition through aggressive textual appropriation . . ." (184-185). Although no two short quotations can give justice to Copeland's complex and detailed arguments about how translation came to empower the vernacular, I believe her ideas can be applied to the *LH*, a compilation of translations used to empower a community, and allow us to construct a more accurate comprehension of the purpose and goals of its compilers as they searched for and translated texts for their project. They were not interested in mere literal translation of any given text, instead, they were interested in appropriating those texts for their own purposes, which as we have seen, involved the development of an ideology of pilgrimage in both theory and practice. This is why reading the translations backwards towards their sources can be interesting and useful, but also distorting if left without further elaboration. One must also ask questions such as Why this text? Why in this specific place in the codex? What strategies were used to achieve a unified whole? When we ask these questions, we stop seeing the codex as a series of translations from French, some more and others less competent, and we begin to see it as a creative[2] and independent work whose unity and internal coherence must be accounted for.

---

[2] I use this word both in our contemporary sense and in the classical understanding pointed out by Copeland: "*Inventio* (Greek *heuresis*) literally means a 'coming upon,' a discovery of that which is there, or already there, to be discovered. The term has little to do with originality or with creation *ex nihilo*" (151). It seems obvious to me that what we perceive as modern creativity on the part of the compilers of the *LH* was the result of a process of discovering and then elucidating that which was already in the texts they chose to translate and order.

CHAPTER VI

STANDARDIZATION OF LANGUAGE:
PERPETUATING THE FRAGMENTATION OF A WHOLE

The key to understanding the language of the *LH* can be found in the introductory words of the tale of the *Santa enperatris* where it is reported that the text was "trasladado en françes / & de françes en gallego" [fol. 99d]. John Maier and I pointed out this important piece of information in 1982 and it remains clear to me that the language of the *LH* is a form of medieval Castilian marked by Galician influence in various forms and lexical items. Furthermore, the language shows this Galician flavor consistently from beginning to end and is clearly the product of the same team or individual. However, by 1982 most of the currently available editions of the various tales were already in print or preparation. Therefore one encounters a variety of ways of describing the language of the texts. In his edition of the *Otas* text Herbert Baird posits an intermediate text between the Castilian codex and the French source:

> De lo que hemos podido observar en el estudio lingüístico de esta obra, en el cual encontramos gran número de formas dialec-tales de usos gramaticales que serían arcaísmos chocantes en el castellano de fines del siglo XIV o principios del siglo XV, te-nemos que inferir que el presente MS de *Otas de Roma* es una copia de otro, posiblemente intermedio entre aquél y la traduc-ción original española en dialecto leonés de la *chanson Florence de Rome*. (9)

One must wonder if he might not have written "dialecto gallego-portugués" had he considered the text of *Otas* to be linked in any way to the *Santa enperatris*.

In his edition of *Santa Maria Egiçiaca* Walker speaks of features that are "clearly western" (xxii) although, as Maier and I pointed out in 1982 (p. 29, n. 20), in several footnotes he mentions "eastern" features (see notes 6, 13, 22, and 23 on pp. 34-36). In his study of the *Egiçiaca* Manuel Alvar mentions examples of both Leonese and Galician, but concludes that "este breve ramillete de pruebas basta para demostrar el carácter leonés de la versión prosificada" (124). In his edition of *Plaçidas* Walker becomes more specific than in the *Egiçiaca* and talks of "features that reflect the western dialects of the Iberian Peninsula, particularly Leonese" (xii). He concludes "that the original compilation was in Leonese or Galician-Portuguese and that MS h-I-13 represents a castilianized later copy" (xv). Benaim de Lasry does not comment at length on the language of her texts, but she does mention the "lost Galician translation" (50) of the *Santa enperatris*, although later she equivocates and states: "It is indeed regrettable that, due to the loss of the Galician translation, if there ever *was* one . . ." (69 her emphasis). Maier limits his comments on the language of the *Gujllelme* to mentioning the fact that "the text has a demonstrable western flavor" (lviii). Rees-Smith, in his edition of the lives of Mary Magdalene and Martha, speaks of the language as "predominantly Castilian, with a sprinkling of non-Castilian (mostly Leonese and Galician-Portuguese) features" (xxxii). He goes on to list the western features of each of the texts he edits concluding that there is evidence to posit two distinct translators at work on the two texts (xxxiv-xxxv).

All editors agree, then, that the texts display varying levels of western elements, yet none is willing to use other texts of the codex as aids in the preparation of the various editions. Indeed, as is the case so often with editorial practices, the evidence actually present in the codex, what Dagenais calls the "physical text" ("Bothersome Residue" 246), is often ignored or doubted (cf. Benaim de Lasry's equivocation noted above) while non-existent, regularized forms are privileged as standard features of the editions.[1]

Let me elaborate with examples from the various editions. One of the best technical or linguistic arguments for editing the whole of

---

[1] See "Bothersome Residue" for more comments on the tradition of giving priority to absence over presence, a process he calls "a flight from presence" (249) following Derrida.

h.I.13 while using conservative editorial criteria can be made from looking at editorial emendations made upon the texts of the *LH*. The verb form *trayo* in the text of *Santa Maria Egiçiaca* on folio 13b is a case in point. The lettering in the MS is smudged and therefore partially illegible (see facsimile of the folio side on page 443, Vol. II of Alvar's edition). Both Walker (27) and Alvar (151) do not mention this situation and have provided the word as *traygo* without comment. However, the first person singular of *traer* throughout the codex is *trayo* (it occurs six times, with one occurence of its preterite homograph). The form *traygo* does not appear in the codex. The first time *trayo* appears other than the case in question is on fol. 40b in the tale of *Rey Gujllelme*, some 27 folios further into the manuscript. Those who edit single tales from the *LH* not only fail to provide the appropriate literary, cultural, and historical context for them, but also are prone to create a language for the tales which cannot be supported by the evidence of the physical text. The result is a situation in which each editor "corrects" or standardizes the language of his/her text in an ad hoc way.

Another example of a questionable emendation from the same portion of the codex was addressed by John Maier and myself in 1982:

> We are reminded of the sentence in *Santa Maria Egiçiaca* which reads: "Entonçe le dixo Zozimas, 'Do es tu, bestia saluaje'" Walker has emended this to: "Entonçe le dixo Zozimas, 'do e[re]s tu, bestia salvaje?'" (p. 30). He notes this emendation and states that the ms reading makes little sense. If we are dealing with a text that shows Western features, as he himself indicates in his introduction (pp. xxii-xxv), and if the ultimate source of these features is a Galician source, as another of the texts indicates, then there is no need for Walker's emendation. As far as we know, *es* is a perfectly acceptable Portuguese and Galician form for the second person singular of the verb 'to be.' (26)

This in 1977. Interestingly enough, by his 1982 edition of the *Plaçidas* text he recognizes the same form as a Galician-Portuguese feature and allows it to stand unemended (see his pp. xiii, 11, and 43, n. 20). However, his recognition of the accuracy of the form does not call upon the evidence of the codex itself since he makes no reference at all to the *Egiçiaca* text and his earlier emendation nor to the occurrence of the same form in the *Cataljna* text (27, 53). It is as if knowledge of the text and its language emerged mysteriously and not in close association with the other tales in the manuscript. Despite, then, his allusion to the unity of the collection where he claims that an emphasis on female suffering allows the *Plaçidas* text to "take its place alongside the other tales in the Escorial MS h-I-13" (xxxv), his actual editorial procedures neither recognize nor honor that unity.

The matter, however, becomes even more complicated. On page 42, notes 17 and 18 he discusses two 'western' forms respectively: the first person singular preterite tense *fue* and the singular imperative *vay*. Walker emends the first of these to *fu[y]* "in the interests of standardization of forms at this point" (note 17), ostensibly because the same form, *fuy*, occurs just five words before the emended instance. One must ask why he felt compelled to standardize the language in this instance and not in the case of *vay*. What standard is used in order to make the emendation? Medieval Castilian? From which period? From which region? Was the Castilian of that period "standardized"? Were there not competing forms vying with one another? A more over-arching question has to do with this urge or need to "standardize" in the first place. I must confess that for me one of the great attractions of studying medieval Spanish has been the beauty and wealth of expression I find in a language that can sustain, for instance, *ande / andodi / andude / anduve* as competing ways of uttering or writing the same semantic notion. I take joy in seeing, reading, and teaching the forms *my* and *amygos*, which Walker has *silently* emended to *mí* (16, l. 6) and *amigos* (18, l. 15) in the *Plaçidas*, despite his statement to the contrary (xliii). Medieval Spanish manuscripts abound in future tense forms in which the endings are split from the roots allowing for an intervening pronoun of the type: *tornar uos hemos*. Why would one choose to present such a form "in accordance with the norms of modern *Portuguese*: e.g. *tornar-vos-hemos*" as Walker does in *Plaçidas* (see xliii, my emphasis)?

On folio 117c-d the tale of *Vna santa enperatriz* reads as follows:

> Mas mucho auia el corasçon fuerte /
> / & entero en sofrir coita & p<ro>uez'a /}
> [fol. 117d]
> por ganar la vida del alma / &'

asi era conplida / dela graçia del
ssanto sp<irit>u q<ue> non amaua njn pre-
çiaua cosa su cue<r>po / njn q<ue>ria conpa-
n~a nin amor de om(~)e / ca bien sabia q<ue> era cosa vana:/.

Anita Benaim de Lasry imposes modern punctuation and accentu-
ation to this text and provides the following reading:

> Mas mucho avía el corasçón fuerte & entero en sofrir coita &
> proveza | [117d] por ganar la vía [sic] del alma. E así era conpli-
> da de la graçia del Santo Spíritu que non amava nin preçiava
> cosa. Su cuerpo nin quería conpaña, nin amor de omne, ca bien
> sabía que era cosa vana. (214)

Quite apart from the fact that she misreads *vida* as *vía* is the fact
that in ignoring the punctuation of the scribe at this point she provides a reading that is possible but highly dubious. By her punctuation "non amava nin preçiava cosa" would mean "She did not love
or cherish anything" with the word *cosa* being interpreted as part of
a negative pair similar to the modern French *non . . . pas*. The following sentence would begin with the double negation that "Her
body neither wanted companionship nor the love of a man . . . ."
Yet it seems clear to me that by following the punctuation of the
codex itself we would get a reading more like: "She neither loved
nor cherished her body at all nor did she want companionship nor
the love of man, for she knew well that such was a vain thing." In
this reading the word *cosa* means "at all" and functions adverbially
instead of having the nominal function suggested in Lasry's reading.
One of the goals of a standardized or regularized text is to ease the
task of reading since it is assumed that lack of modern punctuation
places too many obstacles in the way of the reader. I believe this example shows that just as often modern punctuation serves to mislead the reader and hinder a proper comprehension of the text.

The urge to standardize and modernize also emerges from a
mistrust of what one encounters in the folios of a codex. Let us
look at another example from the *Santa enperatris* text. On folio
118a one encounters the following text which speaks of worldly
wealth and "viçio":

le dixo / Catiua q<ue> as. / esta aue<n>-
tura & esta coita q<ue> sufres / te
veno por tu bien / & gradeçe a
dios esta p<ro>uez'a q<ue> te dio / & la
Riq<ue>z'a q<ue> auias te echo en mal
&' muchas vez'es aviene asy
/ q<ue> echa en mala vent<ur>a aq<ue>llos
q<ue>la mucho Aman / & demas q<ue> da
con<e>llos en<e>l jnfierno / Ca los
mas preçiados & mas rricos / seran p<er>didos. /

Lasry provides the following reading of the text:

> . . . le dixo: '¡Cativa! ¿Qué as? Esta aventura, & esta coita que
> sufresw te veno por tu bien; & gradeçe a Dios esta proveza que
> te dio, & la riqueza que avías te echó en mal.' E muchas vezes
> aviene asy que echa en mala ventura aquellos que la mucho
> aman, & demás queda con ellos en el infierno, ca los más preçia-
> dos & más ricos serán perdidos . . . . (215)

Note that because she mistrusts so strongly what she finds in the
codex itself she ignores the scribe's word break and abuts the verb
form *da* (from *dar*) to *que*, thus providing the word *queda*. One
must assume that the meaning of the sentence thus edited would be
something like "wealth remains in hell with them [those that love it
so much]." The reading with *da*, the correct reading in my opinion,
would mean that "wealth causes them to end up in hell" (that is, it
throws them down into hell). This correct reading is confirmed by
the occurrence of "dar con<e>llos en jnfierno" on fol. 119a, transcribed by Benaim de Lasry as "dar con ellos en infierno . . ." just
two pages later (her page 217). The point remains, however, that
many contemporary editors mistrust what they find in manuscripts
and impose their own readings of texts on their unsuspecting readers. My semi-paleographic edition (and the Hispanic Seminary's
transcription procedures in general) allows readers to choose for
themselves among possible readings of the text.

Let us look at the example of the alternation of the words *boy*
and *buey* for 'ox'. The western form occurs three times, with the
more standard *buey* occuring twice. Would the demands of standardization require that we emend the three occurrences of *boy* to

buey? On folio 31b the two forms occur within two lines of one another, which seems to be as clear an indication as possible that con-
sistency of form was not a matter of high priority among the makers
of this medieval book. Is this not further evidence for what Dagenais has called the "incoherence" of medieval texts (*Ethics*, 16-17)?
Observe likewise the variations of the word *caratulas, carautulas,
caratolas* all on the same folio side (fol. 82r), and the occurrence of
yuntar and *juntar* on successive lines (fol. 52a).

The drive to standardize according to our contemporary ways
of printing and reading, thereby imposing the cadences and
rhythms determined by modern punctuation, capitalization, and indeed orthographic conventions, as well as providing non-existent
words and forms, obliterates the medieval experience of reading
which involved actual physical effort in working out the code. As
Dagenais has pointed out so well in *Ethics* (27 and *passim*), this
physical experience involved stops and starts, mistakes, etc. Standardization also eliminates what Camille has called "sumptuous
reading" ("Philological Iconoclasm" 382). I myself would relate the
physical experience of reading h.I.13 to that of reading avant-garde
free verse such as Huidobro's *Altazor* or Paz's *Piedra de sol*, long
poems in which the reader's participation forms an integral part of
the poetic dynamic. It is also comparable to the free flow of un-
punctuated, stream-of-conscious prose of our own century, language which requires a similar effort on the part of the readers.
That is to say, the individual before the manuscript experiences
something very distinct from that of reading a properly punctuated
and "standardized" text. In rejecting the standardization or mod-
ernization of the language of the *LH* one allows it to display its own
particular cacophony, ungrammaticalness, and chaos, all traits typical of the Middle Ages.[2]

Of course what I am describing here accounts solely for the specific individual who actually interrelated with the codex. One must
imagine a quite varied experience on the part of those hearers who
made up the bulk of the *LH* community, whose reactions must have
ranged from boredom and distraction to absolute enthrallment
with the story being "read." Obviously, for this contingent much

---

[2] See Menocal for a brilliant discussion of the notions of cacophony and ungrammaticalness in the Middle Ages as opposed to the ordered "Master Narrative"
of the modern period.

depended on the talent of the individual doing the "performance" and handling the codex. This relationship between orality and textuality, however one may see it, need not be agreed upon in order to recognize the value of producing an edition of the whole codex before embarking on editorial procedures that tamper with the "physical text."

Each portion of the *LH* has been edited at different times by editors using different and arbitrary standardization, or what Baird calls "regularización de la grafía" (9). He claims, for instance, to have followed "un plan moderado" (*ibid.*) of such regularization since he seems interested in "hacer resaltar un poco más el sabor antiguo del texto" (10). That must mean that he is not producing a "modernized" version of the text in the tradition of an "odres nuevos" edition. The most lamentable result of such practices has been the fact that the fragmentation of the *LH* has become the rule. Editions of its various parts have been produced, given titles, studied vis-à-vis their source texts, and provided with both philological and historical contexts. The process establishes such texts as received or canonical even if, in fact, the texts edited are only portions of a whole. This is even more so if the editions produced in this way are received by the profession with favorable or even not-so-favorable reviews. The result is a distortion opposite but comparable to what Dagenais has pointed out for the *LBA* in *Ethics* and "Bothersome Residue."

CHAPTER VII

A REVIEW OF MODERN EDITIONS

In this section I propose to review the various modern editions
of the tales that make up the *LH*. In this review I shall indicate
areas and sections where previous editions show paleographic inac-
curacies and where portions of text have been mistranscribed. In
many of these cases I shall be able to show conclusively that the errors could have been avoided had the codex as a whole been used
as a guide by the various editors. I shall also indicate those points at
which lines of the text have been eliminated by homeoteleuton.

1. EDITIONS OF *SANTA MARIA MAGDALENA* AND *SANTA MARTA*

The editions of Michel and Ruggieri are difficult to obtain and
therefore I shall not include them in this review. Suffice it to say
that Michel's introductory study and her notes to the two texts are
often perceptive and very useful, as I have indicated above in the
discussion of the unity of the codex.

The two remaining editions, both from the latter half of the
1980's, are accurate renditions of the manuscript. In the case of the
Walsh/Thompson edition (W/T) I would point out that they consistently transcribe *muger* for a word that occurs only as *mugier*
when it is written without abbreviation. Rees Smith (RS) does not
present this problem. However, he eliminates approximately two
thirds of a line of text on the very first folio of the codex, his page
number 3, line 8 reads: "Marta e con aquel çiego . . ." but should
read "Marta e con *su hermano sant lazaro* & aquel çiego. . . ." Both
texts provide the word *todo* (W/T, page 28, line 32; RS page 5, line

16) for what is clearly *çedo* in the codex. On page 7, line 9 RS renders *folgaredes* for what is clearly *folgardes* in the codex. This is an important distortion since the syncopated form is another example of western features. Both editions emend the manuscript's *bretaña* to *B(r)etaña* (W/T at page 37, line 400; RS at page 37, line 13). Are editors justified in imposing this kind of correction, basing themselves on source texts (W/T on a Latin text; RS on a French one) without considering that for both compilers and readers *bretaña* might be a more meaningful and therefore more correct reading? (See Morrás' review of RS, at page 120; she is equally doubtful concerning this emendation.) RS, page 41, line 23 and 47, line 13 provides *tenya* where the codex reads *t<ra>ya*. The scribal abbreviation for the graphs -ra- is consistent and clear throughout the manuscript, yet it seems to bewilder a number of contemporary editors who provide erroneous resolutions for the abbreviation and therefore establish linguistic forms and a text that have never existed. W/T provide the form *oviera* on page 39, line 449 for what is clearly *ouiese*, and on the same page, line 490, they provide the form *Jermán* for the manuscript's *jepnan*.

2. EDITIONS OF *SANTA MARIA EGIÇIACA*

Knust's edition of 1890 is difficult to locate and has been superseded by the more contemporary editions of Alvar and Walker. These two editions are complementary in the sense that Alvar's pretends to be a paleographic edition whereas Walker's is a "reading" edition which imposes standardization of language and contemporary punctuation, capitalization and accents.

Alvar's edition is flawed by misreadings of letters, skipping of words, and misnumbering of lines. The first two flaws are rather serious in an edition that claims paleographic accuracy; the third flaw results from the first two, but is rather irritating in the sense that it seems ludicrous to count lines if one is going to do so inaccurately.

Let us dispense with the case of skipped text since it occurs only once on the folio Alvar numbers 10r., col. at the line he numbers 30. His line reads: "leda, Et non era fea, ca mucho fazia aspra". In fact, there are two lines which read: "leda / &' non era marauilla si ella 'era fea / ca mucho fazia aspra". This error causes him to present 34 lines of text where in fact there are 35, a count that can be confirmed on page 437 of vol. 2 of his edition where the manuscript folios are reproduced in facsimile.

Other folio columns to have lines misnumbered are 8a, 8b, 13b, and 14a. In all four cases he combines two lines of text into one thereby throwing off the line count by minus 1.

Misreadings are relatively numerous for a paleographic edition. The most serious involves the word *mugier*, which Alvar presents as *mugi<er>*. That is, he reads the letters that are actually written by the scribe as *mugi* and adds *er* as his resolution of the abbreviation. In fact, the letters actually written by the scribe are *mugr*, as can be confirmed by looking at column 13a in the facsimile that Alvar provides on page 443, vol. 2 of his edition. There it can be clearly observed that the final letter of the word in question on line 28 is exactly the same as the final letter of the Latin word *noster* on line 32 and of the final letter in *señor* on line 35. In fact, the scribal practice throughout the manuscript is very consistent concerning the word *mugier*.

On folio 7d, line 5, Alvar reads *q<ui>sie<r>edes* for what is clearly *q<ue>sie<r>edes* in the codex. The practice of distinguishing the general mark of suppression which represents *<ue>* from the more vertical mark that represents *<u>i`* is consistent and clear throughout the whole of the manuscript. As with the abbreviated *<ra>* of *traya* above, what we have here is a difficulty on the part of many editors in reading superscript letters.

Folio 8c at line 31 provides the form *ergureyon* for what is clearly *erguyeron* in the manuscript. Again, the form can be confirmed by consulting Alvar's facsimile. Alvar reads the word *jnfierno* twice as *ynfierno* (fols. 9c12 and 16), mistaking the letter *j* for *y*, despite the fact that the *y* typically preferred by the hand of h.I.13 can be seen just one folio before on 9b7 in the word *ymagen* (page 436 of the facsimile). At folio 10d30 Alvar reads *egl<esi>a* for the abbreviated form *eglā*. In all other cases in the codex the abbreviated form provides the *j*: *egljā* (there are 45 occurrences). The western form *egleja* appears once in the life of St. Martha at fol. 6c. Since the standard form is usually written with a long *j*, with its abbreviation representing solely *es*, it is more prudent in this case to transcribe the word as *egl<es>a*, a possible intermediate form. The tilde above the word *mjnjñez* on fol. 11d13 is ignored by Alvar, thus he provides the word *mininez*. At stake is another possible western or Gallician form, as with several other words whose tildes have been ignored by modern editors (e.g., *coñocer, reyña*, etc.). At folio 12b32 and 33 Alvar reads *q<ue>resma* for the same combination of letters and mark of suppression that he renders as *q<ua>resma* just five lines later at 12c2 and 3. The word is clearly *q<u>a`resma*, and what is causing trouble for the editor is once again the issue of a superscript letter. At folio 12d34 Alvar reads *desamparado* where the scribe has clearly written *desanparado*. Not only is *n* the graph preferred throughout the manuscript for a nasal before bilabials, but, indeed, it is clearly the letter in this example. Alvar seems to interpret the initial stroke of the *p* as one of the verticals of an *m*; it is not. At 13a31 Alvar provides the odd Creed "*credo nj deum*" for what is clearly *jn*. Finally, the reader is reminded of the silently reconstructed verb form *traygo* which should be *trayo* at what Alvar numbers as fol. 13r., col. b21 (see above, section VII).

Walker's 1977 edition is intended as a reading text and has been regularized in a variety of ways (see above, section VI). However, except for three words of text omitted it is a more accurate transcription of the tale than Alvar's. The omission occurs at page 12, line 9 which reads: "oyó la misa e adoró la cruz. E después que" and should read: "oyó la misa e adoró la cruz syn njngunt destoruo. E después que". On page 11, line 8 (and note 14) Walker emends a word he claims is *fiste* to *f[u]ste*. If one uncurls the parchment at that point the word *fuste* can be seen quite clearly. His emendation and note are pointless. At page 13, line 3 Walker reads the abbreviated *pº* as *por*. It should read *p<rimer>o`*. At page 16, line 9 (and note 19) *ordo* should read *ordjo*. Walker's note 19 mentions "a faint vertical stroke between final *d* and *o*", but rejects it as a scribal interpolation. I believe it to be legitimate. At page 16, line 26 Walker reads *eglesia* for what I believe should be transcribed as *eglesa* (see my comments concerning the same word in Alvar's edition).

3. EDITIONS OF *SANTA CATALJNA*

The only edition other than my own of the life of Santa Cataljna is Knust's version published in 1890. Contemporary philology and transcription norms have made his practices look arbitrary. For example, he eliminates all cedillas before e and i, thereby distorting the forms that are actually written in the codex. He reads sigmas only as s, thus providing forms such as *pas* for *paz* (page 232, line

5); *fasian* for *fazian* (232, 9); *dies* for *diez* (232, 12; *fiso* for *fizo* (232, 12), etc. There are countless errors of transcription such as page 234, line 6 *muriesen* which should read *moriesen* and page 234, line 21 *ayuntaron* which should read *ajuntaron*, and so forth throughout the edition. In addition, there are two points at which he eliminates text per homeoteleuton: page 274, line 3 reads "echarla en una carcel otra ves" and should read "echarla en una carcel mucha escura & asy fue la virgen en carcel otra ves." Page 307, line 5 reads: "gloriosa nacencia e por tristesa" and should read "gloriosa nacencia e por morrer gozo & por llorar lediçia & por tristesa." On the other hand, Knust knew this codex well and his readings clearly saved me from embarrassment on several occasions. I prefer to look at my version as a collaboration with the work of this esteemed German Hispanist. In addition to providing the text from h.I.13, Knust provides both the French and Latin versions of the saint's life.

4. Editions of *El Cavallero Plaçidas*

Knust's edition of 1878 is difficult to find and will not be considered here. Walker's 1982 edition is the standard edition in our profession. It is a relatively trustworthy text except for two lines of the manuscript that have been eliminated by homeoteleuton. The first of these is at page 32, line 4 which reads: "desy contóle más todas las cosas por que Jheso Christo" and should read: "desy contóle como le ajenjera & contole más todas las cosas por que Jhesu Christo." The second line eliminated is at page 40, line 8 which reads: "tienpo fezieron su fiesta dos días andados de" but should read: "tienpo fezieron sobre ellos vna capilla & fezieron su fiesta dos días andados de."

MS h.I.13 abounds in forms of *conocer / desconocer / reyna / reyno*, etc. that bear a tilde above the nasal. Most editors have eliminated what they considered to be a superfluous mark. Given the western nature of the language, however, I believe it prudent to represent the palatalized consonant. Forms of this nature can be found at page 3, line 4 (*desconoçer*); page 7, line 9 (*conosçieses*); page 10, line 10 (*conosçieran*); page 24, line 3 (*conosco*); and page 25, line 10 (*conosçer*). In all these cases the words should be transcribed with an *ñ*.

At page 6, line 4 Walker reads *capos* for *ca<n>pos*. The tilde is present in the codex. On the same page at line 15 he reads *otro* for what is clearly *ot<r>i`*, a form that occurs five other times in the codex (fols. 34c; 47a; 88c; 100d; 143b). At page 10, line 4 he reads *quantos* for *q<u>i`tos* as per his own transcription of *quitados*, page 32, line 19 where he resolves the same abbreviation correctly. At issue yet again is the inability of contemporary editors to appreciate the distinction between horizontal and vertical marks of suppression consistently. In h.I.13 vertical abbreviations invariably indicate the superscript vowel *i*.

At page 10, line 6 Walker reads *buen* for what is *bien* in the MS. Conversely, on page 25, line 20 he reads *bien* for *buen*. On page 12, line 22 *piensas* should read *pienses*. And at page 18, line 7 *conpaña* should read *conpanja*. At page 19, line 3 Walker presents the emended *plug[u]ier*. I myself would be cautious since there are three other occurrences of the same form: *plugier / plogier* at fols. 46b; 132c; and 146d, as well as forms such as *njeges* where one would expect *njegues* (see below, review of Editions of *Carlos Maynes*). In addition, the codex registers other non-standard forms such as *ploglier*, see folio 110d. On page 24, line 14 Walker reads *rrectaron* for *Recataron* and page 28, line 1 exhibits the printing error *desques* for *despues*.

5. Editions of *El Rrey Gujllelme*

Again, Knust's 1878 publication is difficult to locate and inadequate philologically. I shall proceed to the 1984 edition of Maier. Gumpert has pointed out in his review that the text is flawed by the omission of a large number of manuscript lines which he proceeds to provide. I would add the following erroneous readings. At page 4, line 1 *setemo* should read *setymo*; page 5, line 2 *maytines* should read *matynes*; page 6, line 24 *avimos* should read *ovjmos*; page 7, line 22 *echades* should read *echedes*; page 11, line 23 *desanparada* should read *desanparadera*; page 12, line 18 *arlortar* should read *arlotar*; page 13, line 1 *demando* should read *demande*; page 13, line 20 reads *grant pesar e fue corriendo* should read *grant pesar e fue en pos el corriendo*; page 18, line 18 *a que* should read *a qui,* again the vertical mark of suppression being misread as in so many other instances; page 24, line 21 *tolhestes* should read *tolliestes*; page 28, line 9 *ya* should read *ja*; page 29, line 19 *llamole* should read *lamolo*; page 34, line 7 *madrugada* should read *madurgada*; page 51, line 8 *porque la toller* should read *por ge la toller*.

6. EDITIONS OF *OTAS DE ROMA*

Amador's nineteenth-century edition is available in the reprint of his literary history, but its philological accuracy is not always dependable. I shall limit my comments to Baird's edition of 1976. It is one of the more reliable transcriptions of h.I.13. This is especially fortunate since the *Otas* text is by far the longest tale in the collection (it runs for over 50 of the manuscripts 151+ folios). Baird has omitted a few lines of the text which will be presented here, and he misreads a handful of words which will also be corrected below. The most disappointing aspect of the transcription is his insistence in transcribing *muger* for the abbreviated *mug̃r* whose full form, *mugier*, occurs twice in this section of the manuscript: page 99, line 8 and page 102, line 13 of Baird's text. Both of these occurrences are transcribed correctly by Baird and should have been used as a basis for a more accurate transcription of the abbreviated forms. Baird regularizes the language and thus provides, for instance, *v* for *u* when it represents a consonantal sound (see page 36, line 24 *avia* for what is *auja* in the codex). Likewise *v* when representing a vowel is regularized to *u*, thus the manuscript's *vno* becomes *uno* in his edition (see, for instance, page 36, line 25). Vocalic *j* is always edited to *i*, etc. We have seen above (section VI) that Baird desired to preserve and privilege to some extent the "sabor antiguo" of the text. How one achieves that goal while tampering with the language is a mystery to me.

Baird has omitted the following words or lines of text. At page 17, lines 11 and 12, Baird provides *E levavan treynta cavallos . . .* which should read *E leuauan cauallos & armas frescas que Reluzian al sol & leuauan treynta cauallos. . . .* Page 20, line 11 reads: *nos puede ayudar* and should read *nos puede bien ayudar*. On the same page, line 23 reads: *non quesieron y mas estar. E* and should read *non quesieron y mas estar & fueron su carrera. E*. At page 24, line 36 *E commo era* should read *E de commo era*. Page 23, line 34 reads *muy sabroso* and should read *muy bueno & sabroso*. Page 24, line 34 reads *ricos paños de oro* and should read *ricos paños de seda a ban-*

das enque eran figurados quinze paños de oro. Page 25, line 10 reads *muy granada mente, ca* and should read *muy granada mente a mi gente ca.* Page 36, line 12 reads *que trayan por engeño* and should read *que trayan sobre vn carro que trayan por engeño.* Page 39, line 7 reads *piedras por el* and should read *piedras preçiosas por el.* Page 40, line 34 reads *conel en tierra* and should read *conel del cauallo en tierra.* Page 41, line 38 reads *non quiero encobrir* and should read *non quiero yo encobrir.* Page 45, line 8 reads *el viejo Garsir* and should read *el viejo de Garsir.* Page 46, line 26 reads *enperador, ca* and should read *enperador otas, ca.* Page 59, line 21 reads *Tomad* and should read *señor tomad.* Page 68, line 3 reads *E el apostoligo dio* and should read *E el apostoligo le dio.* Page 78, line 18 reads *e que metiesen* and should read *e que los metiesen.* Page 103, line 2 reads *averedes en* and should read *aueredes vos en.* Page 114, line 24 reads *non avia culpa* and should read *non avia y culpa.*

In addition, I list here those cases where my readings differ from Baird's. On page 13 in the title of the text he reads *buen cavallero Esmere* and I read *buen cauallero esmero.* On page 19, line 8 Baird reads *Garssyr* where the MS reads *gerssir.* At page 31, line 36 Baird provides: *E p[or que].* The text reads *& pues*; there is no need for his reconstruction at this point. On page 32, line 14 Baird reads *maravillame* for what I see as *marauillome.* On the same page at line 15 he reads *çien* for the manuscript's *çient.* On page 38, line 16 Baird reads *Saria* for what is *siria* in the codex. On line 34 of the same page he reads *cav'el* for *fauel* (*berart fauel* would be a name very similar to *felipe fauuel* – Baird transcribes *Fauvel* – on page 39, line 4). Baird's *Esmeré* on page 64, line 35 should read *Esmery.* On page 66, line 35 *ally* should read *assy.* Page 77, line 37 reads *non avera y* and should read *non Aueria y.* At page 88, line 10 Baird transcribes the word *muesy* for what looks to me to be a repetition of the word *mueso* ('bit on a horse bridle') that occurs just one line above in the codex. In this second case there is a ligature from the tall *s* to the following *o* which may have been interpreted by Baird as a *y.* On the same page on line 32 *troxo* should read *traxo.* Page 92, line 37 *Parad vos demi* should read *partid vos de mi.* On page 94, line 4 Baird provides the form *cochiello* for what I see as *cochillo.* Page 96, line 20 reads *fallaron* for *fallaran.* At page 101, line 3 Baird provides the word *otra* for what I see as *ot<r>i`.* Baird joins the many editors who fail to represent the superscript *i.* Two lines later he reads *assy* for *ally.* On the same page at line 14 *llevaron* should read *leuaron*. Baird provides the form *almondear* on page 104, line 24 where I would read *almonedear*. At page 109, line 18 the text reads *cuando* where it should provide the medieval form *quando*. This is probably a typesetter's error. Page 117, line 18 shows *era* where I see *auia*. This ends the divergent readings between our two transcriptions.

7. EDITIONS OF *VNA SANTA ENPERATRIS*

The nineteenth-century edition by Mussafia is out of date and difficult to locate. I shall therefore limit my comments to the 1982 edition of Benaim de Lasry. The edition is flawed by inaccurate transcription from beginning to end. It seems evident to me that Benaim de Lasry used a microfilm in the preparation of the edition and that she often could not see exactly what was written on the folios. However, her problems are not limited to that difficulty since she also proposes certain erroneous transcription norms such as her failure to distinguish between the usual mark of abbreviation and the superscript *i* (see page 111 for her discussion of *que* and *qui*). An example of this problem, common to many of the editors of texts from h.I.13 would be her transcription of *ot<r>i`* as *otro* on page 179, line 18. Benaim de Lasry claims always to show a cedilla when it is written in the manuscript, yet on the same page I have noted three times in which she has missed a cedilla: line 2 *cielos* should read *çielos*; line 24 *apercebido* should read *aperçebido*; and line 25 *necio* should read *neçio*. On the same page yet again, she misses four words of text. Line 4 reads in part: *alma oviese gualardon* and should read *alma ende ouiese gualardon*. At line 9 and 10 the text reads *a Dios & su mugier* and should read *a dios & a su mugier*. Line 19 reads in part *que era loada* and should read *que era ende loada*. Finally, at line 23 the text reads *poderia fallar* and should read *poderia om(~)e fallar*. Footnote 8 at the bottom of the page: "*ca*: should be *que*" is erroneous since throughout the whole of h.I.13 *ca* is occasionally used as a comparative conjunction equivalent to the more usual *que* 'than' (see Baird 188). This kind of footnote is possible when separate editions of the various tales are published by editors unfamiliar with the codex as a whole. One must be grateful in this case that Benaim de Lasry limited her comment to a footnote and did not take it upon herself to regularize or standardize the text. At lines 20 and 28 the pronoun that Benaim de Lasry reads as *la* (*la fazia* and *la plaz*) I see as *le* in both cases.

On page 192 the editor reconstructs *sus[teng]ades* from what she must read as *susades*. In fact, what is written in the manuscript is *ssufrades*, a word which fits quite appropriately in the context. The *f* and *r* are connected by a ligature that give the impression of a long *s* followed by a *t*. I would imagine this to be particularly confusing if one reads the text from a microfilm. On the last two lines of page 202 Benaim de Lasry provides the following words: "*que por pavor de muerte quiera perder mi candor & mi alma.*" The word she sees as *candor* is actually *c<r>i`ador;* she mistakes the superscript *i* that is clearly written on the folio for a general mark of suppression.

On page 203 the empress is threatened with being thrown overboard if she does not sexually satisfy the retinue of sailors on Escot's ship. The empress calls upon Mary for aid. Lasry provides the following text:

> E la madre de Dios, que bien la oyó, los fizo asy estar pasmados, que se tenneron de la echar en la mar.

In her introductory study she quotes exactly this text and compares it to the French source:

> 1885   La mere Dieu qui bien l'oï
> Les mariniers si esbloï
> E mist en els tele fraor,
> De li noier orent poor (63)

She states: "Due to the omission of the important line 1887 – indicating the seamen's fear of the divine – the motive of the vilain's [*sic*] hesitation is not clearly depicted in the Spanish text" (*ibid.*). Judging from the text provided by Lasry one would have to agree that the concept of fear is lacking in the Spanish version. However, one might ask just exactly what is meant by the word *tenneron*. Unfortunately, the word is not listed in Lasry's glossary despite the fact that it must look odd to all speakers of Spanish. In fact, what we have here is an error in transcription that leads to an equally erroneous editorial judgment in which we are told that the Spanish romance is "not as clear . . . as . . . is . . . the original . . . because of an excessive abbreviation" (*ibid*.). The word in question is clearly *temieron* (see fol. 112a) and thus provides the exact meaning that Lasry claims is missing.

I shall provide no further examples. Suffice it to say that the text provided in the edition under consideration is seriously flawed, which as a consequence often weakens the editor's interpretive work to say nothing of how it would mislead the unsuspecting reader. The interested reader is referred to the reviews of Benaim de Lasry's edition by Bershatin, Green, Walker, and myself listed in the bibliography.

8. EDITIONS OF *CARLOS MAYNES*

The editions of both Amador and Bonilla are readily available, at least in libraries, but they have been superseded by at least one of the more modern editions. I shall limit my comments, therefore, to the editions of Benaim de Lasry and Tiemann.

The comments made above about Benaim de Lasry's *Santa enperatris* text concerning the inaccuracy of transcription can be applied equally to her rendition of the *Carlos Maynes* text. Her knowledge of the codex is so minimal that she claims that the four-folio lacuna in the text between folios 142 and 143 "is not noticeable" and that "one would have to be familiar with the story to notice it" (109). Indeed, she claims "it is not a case of missing folios, for the foliation follows consecutively without interruption" (109-110). In fact, the codex exhibits two numerations, one in arabic numerals (the foliation followed by Lasry) and another, the more accurate, in roman numerals (see Maier and Spaccarelli 18-20 and Rees-Smith xxix). In addition, the lacuna she sees as "not noticeable" has been recovered, and a recent study has demonstrated the importance of this lost material (Spaccarelli, "Recovering"). It would be repetitive and unnecessary to list the many errors committed in this edition. The reader is refered to the reviews listed above under *Vna santa enperatris*.

Tiemann's 1977 edition of the *Carlos Maynes* text is the most acceptable rendition of any text from h.I.13 available up until now. He presents a relatively accurate transcription of the manuscript, refrains from adding modern punctuation and standardization, provides the punctuation actually written by the medieval scribes, and recovers the four-folio lacuna between folios 142 and 143 from the 1532 edition of the *Hystoria de la Reyna Seuilla* published in Seville by Cromberger. Unfortunately, Tiemann worked with a photographic version of the manuscript and with the earlier editions of Amador and Bonilla:

> Den Inhalt der Sammelhandschrift hat José Amador de los Rios beschrieben und eine Analyse unseres Cuento gegeben. Derselbe Gelehrte hat auch die erste Ausgabe des Cuento veranstaltet. Verbessert wurde der Text von Adolfo Bonilla y San Martín herausgegeben. Unser Text wurde nach einer Photographie der Handschrift revidiert und neu interpungiert. Der Abweichungen von Bonillas Text sind so viele, dass sie nicht im einzelnen charakterisiert werden können. (18-19)

This procedure has led to several serious misreadings which will be indicated below. Tiemann was most interested in comparing the Old Spanish version of the *Carlos Maynes* story with versions from other European languages; he had little interest in the other tales of h.I.13. As in the case of other scholars who edit single texts from the codex in isolation Tiemann makes errors that could have been avoided had he known the complete manuscript. These cases will be indicated below. The most disappointing aspect of Tiemann's transcription is his decision to transcribe *mug̃r* as *muger* despite the presence of the full form *mugier* in the *Carlos Maynes* section of the codex (see his page 46, line 11).

My readings differ from Tiemann's in the following cases. On page 33, line 14 *escuchat* should read *ascuchat* and on line 23 *catadura* should read *c<r>i`atura*. Line 24 presents an occurrence of *catadura* and it is not at all the same word as on line 23. Yet again superscript letters and vertical marks of suppression cause difficulty for modern editors, especially when working from microfilm. At page 41, line 1 Tiemann's *auria* should read *aueria* and on line 34 *langre* should read *sangre* and *goteua* should read *goteaua*. On page 43, line 3 *commenço* should read *començo*; line 5 *faria* should read *fazia*; and line 11 *y* should read *yr*. Page 44, line 30 has another occurrence of *y* which should read *yo*. On page 45, line 21 *vusso* should read *vusco* and at line 26 *da-le-ha* should read *dar le ha*. Page 46, line 17 *deziean* should read *dezian*. On page 49, line 3 Tiemann transcribes *era* for *ora* and at line 28 he provides *quel* for what is clearly *q<u>a'l* with a superscript *a*. On page 51, line 7 Tiemann's *guardar* should read *guiar* (what is written is a vertical mark instead of the ¨ (superscript *a*). On line 8 of the same page Tiemann reads *c<r>i̇'o* as *tanto*, as have all previous editors. Again, at issue is the vertical mark of suppression which editors often ignore. However, it is hard for me to imagine how one would see *tanto* in the letters actually present in the codex: *c̃o* or *t̃o*. I believe we have an instance here in which a troublesome reading causes editors to go back to previous editions for help in interpreting the evidence of the codex. This process leads them in a kind of domino process to the first edition of the text (in this case Amador's) where we can usually locate the origin of the erroneous reading. Let me hasten to add that I, too, participate in this process, and point it out here not to find fault with other editors, but rather in an effort to locate the origin of the error.

On page 53 line 35 Tiemann provides *mando commo* which should read *mando asy commo*. Page 54, line 35 reads *y* and should read *yo*. On page 55, line 7 *fue* should read *fuer*; line 13 *dixiera* should read *dixieran*; line 14 *esto* should read *este*; and line 27 *juiçio* should read *juizio*. Page 56, line 7 presents *gania* which should read *gana*. At page 58, line 3 *des* should read *del*, and on line 21 *fuera* should read *seria*. Page 61, line 4 has the printing error *guanto* for *quanto* and on line 6 Tiemann reads *comprar* where I have expanded the abbreviation as *comp<rende>r*. At page 63, line 6 Tiemann reads *tener* where I see *t<r>a`er*, another case in which a superscript is misread.

On page 66, line 22 Tiemann reads *guaria* where I see *guarira*. On page 67, line 26 he presents *dizeno* where I read *dozeno*. Page 68, line 25 reads *y* and should read *yo*. On page 71, line 6 I read Tiemann's *agora* as *aq<u>i`* – with a superscript *i* – as on page 81, line 1 where I see *ot<r>i`* for Tiemann's *otro*. Page 83, line 21 reads *pariose* and should read *partiose*. On page 84, line 6 *dire* should read *dare*; line 7 *creer* should read *crer*; line 13 *terna* should read *ternan*; line 27 *Bregona* should read *bregoña*; and line 35 *ploga* should read *plega*. On page 86, lines 16-17 I see only one occurrence of the word *agora* where Tiemann provides the word twice. On page 87, line 28 the word *y* should read *yo*. Page 88, line 17 reads *mando su hueste* and should read *mando venir su hueste*; line 23 *niegues* should read *njeges* – there are a surprisingly large number of forms of this type that eliminate the *u* that modern speakers of Spanish expect (see the review of Editions of *El cavallero Plaçidas* above for comments on *plugier* and *plogier*). On page 90, line 30 Tiemann's *maravedis* should read *m<arc>oˋs* since it is the only monetary denomination used in a full form throughout the manuscript, including three occurrences in the *Carlos Maynes* text which Tiemann himself provides at pages 59, line 6; 86, line 35; and 106, line 25.

Page 92, line 24 reads *lieua* and should read *lieuan* and the word *y* on the same line should read *yo*. At page 93, line 7 Tiemann provides *tirale* for what I read as *tirate*. On page 94, line 6 *sedes* should read *seredes*. Page 100, line 14 *do* should read *dolo*. *Bien* on page 104, line 20 should read *buen* and on lines 27-28 *puso le çinquenta mill maravedis de rrenta* should read *puso le en tierra mill marcos de Renta*, a serious discrepancy indeed. Again, I believe Tiemann's error can be traced all the way back to Amador whose reading has been followed by all three of the other previous editors of the text. The words in question are barely legible on the parchment when viewing it in person at El Escorial, hence Tiemann can be forgiven his misreading based as it is on a microfilm. However, had he used the codex as a whole as a guide for his work he would have perhaps avoided repeating this misreading since at the end of the *Rey Gujllelme* story in a context quite similar to that of the *Carlos Maynes*, the various commoner helpmates are rewarded, one case reporting that the king "alos mercadores puso en tierra mill marcos de Renta cada / año . . ." [fol. 48a]. My comparison of the two portions of text convinces me that the scribe(s) wrote the same words in the two locations.

Finally, on page 106, line 19 Tiemann's *dico* should read *dixo*. At line 34 the last word of the codex is not <par> but rather *p[ar]tir* – one cannot see the bar of suppression through the lower stroke of the *p*, but the three letters *tir* are clear enough when viewing the codex in person. I believe my reconstruction of the word is correct. This last folio is in a state of extreme mutilation.

9. CONCLUSION

My principal purpose in this review of previous editions has not been to publicize the paleographic and editorial errors of the individuals who prepared the various texts; rather I have tried to show how isolated editions of portions of the codex perpetuate the erroneous view that the *LH* is a miscellany of independent works that at best have tangential or marginal relationships to one another. The more technical and philological matters considered here indicate a unified text as clearly as does the literary analysis of the various tales presented above.

CHAPTER VIII

LIST OF WORKS CITED

1. EDITION OF THE *LIBRO DE LOS HUESPEDES*

Spaccarelli, Thomas D., ed. *Text and Concordance of "El Libro de los huespedes" (Escorial MS. h.I.13)*. Madison: Hispanic Seminary of Medieval Studies, 1996.

2. EDITIONS OF PORTIONS OF THE *LIBRO DE LOS HUESPEDES*

(under each sub-section editions are listed in chronological order)

A. *Editions of* Santa Maria Madalena *and* Santa Marta

Michel, Sister Eleanore, ed. *"Vidas de Santa Maria Madalena y Santa Marta" an Edition of the Old Spanish Text*. Diss. U of Chicago, 1930.
Ruggieri, Jole. "Frammenti castigliani delle leggende di SS. Marta e Maddalena," *Archivum Romanicum*, 17 (1933): 189-204.
Walsh, J. K. and B. Bussell Thompson, eds. *The Myth of the Magdalen in Early Spanish Literature (with an edition of the Vida de Santa Maria Madalena in MS. h-I-13 of the Escorial Library)*. New York: Lorenzo Clemente, 1986. [Despite the title, both lives are edited.]
Rees Smith, John, ed. *The Lives of St Mary Magdalene and St Martha (MS Esc. h-I-13)*. Exeter: U of Exeter P, 1989.

B. *Editions of* Santa Maria Egiçiaca

Knust, Hermann, ed. *Geschichte der Legenden der h. Katharina von Alexandrien und der h. Maria Aegyptiaca*. Halle: Niemeyer, 1890: 315-346.
Alvar, Manuel, ed. *Vida de Santa María Egiciaca: Estudios, vocabulario, edición de los textos*. Madrid: Clásicos Hispánicos (CSIC), 1972. 2 vols. Vol. 2: 151-167.
Walker, Roger, ed. *Estoria de Santa María Egiçiaca (MS Escurialense h-I-13)*. 2nd edition. Exeter: U of Exeter, 1977.

C. Editions of Santa Catalina

Knust, Hermann, ed. *Geschichte der Legenden der h. Katharina von Alexandrien und der h. Maria Aegyptiaca.* Halle: Niemeyer, 1890: 232-314.

D. Editions of Plaçidas

Knust, Hermann, ed. *Dos obras didácticas y dos leyendas.* Madrid: Sociedad de Bibliófilos, 1878: 123-157.
Walker, Roger M., ed. *El cavallero Plaçidas (MS Esc. h-I-13).* Exeter: U of Exeter, 1982.

E. Editions of El Rey Guillelme

Knust, Hermann, ed. *Dos obras didácticas y dos leyendas.* Madrid: Sociedad de Bibliófilos, 1878: 172-247.
Maier, John R., ed. *El RRey Guillelme.* Exeter: U of Exeter, 1984.

F. Editions of Otas de Roma

Amador de los Ríos, José, ed. *Historia crítica de la literatura española,* V. Madrid: Imprenta a cargo de José Fernández Cancela, 1864: 391-468.
Baird, Herbert L., Jr., ed. *Análisis lingüístico y filológico de Otas de Roma.* Madrid: Anejos del BRAE, 1976.

G. Editions of De vna santa enperatris

Mussafia, Adolph., ed. "Eine altspanische Prosadarstellung der Crescentiasaga," in *Sitzungsberichte der Kaiserlichen Akademie der Wissenschaften, philosophisch-historische Klasse,* 53 (1867): 499-562.
Benaim de Lasry, Anita, ed. *"Carlos Maynes" and "La enperatrís de Roma": Critical Edition and Study of Two Medieval Spanish Romances.* Newark, Delaware: Juan de la Cuesta, 1982: 177-226.

H. Editions of Carlos Maynes

Amador de los Ríos, José, ed. *Historia crítica de la literatura española,* V. Madrid: Edición a cargo de José Fernández Cancela, 1864: 344-391.
Bonilla y San Martín, Adolfo, ed. *Libros de caballerías.* NBAE, 6, Vol. I. Madrid: Bailly/Bailliere, 1907: 503-533.
Tiemann, Hermann, ed. *Der Roman von der Königin Sibille.* Hamburg: Dr. Ernst Hauswedell & Co., 1977: 33-106.
Benaim de Lasry, Anita, ed. *"Carlos Maynes" and "La enperatrís de Roma": Critical Edition and Study of Two Medieval Spanish Romances.* Newark, Delaware: Juan de la Cuesta, 1982: 113-173.

3. GENERAL STUDIES

Alonso, Martín. *Enciclopedia del idioma*. Madrid: Aguilar, 1958. 3 vols.

Alvar, Manuel, ed. *Vida de Santa María Egiciaca: Estudios, vocabulario, edición de los textos*. Madrid: Clásicos Hispánicos (CSIC), 1972. 2 vols. Vol. I: Estudios.

Benaim de Lasry, Anita. "Narrative Devices in Fourteenth-Century Spanish Romances." *La Corónica* 11 (1983): 280-285.

Bershatin, Israel. Rev. of *"Carlos Maynes" and "La enperatrís de Roma": Critical Edition and Study of Two Medieval Spanish Romances*. Ed. Anita Benaim de Lasry. *Speculum* 59 (1984): 114-117.

Bloch, R. Howard. "Medieval Misogyny and the Invention of Western Romantic Love." *Modernité au moyen âge: Le défi du passé*. Ed. Brigitte Cazelles and Charles Méla. Geneva: Droz, 1990. 289-313.

Blumenfeld-Kosinski, Renate and Timea Szell, eds. *Images of Sainthood in Medieval Europe*. Ithaca: Cornell UP, 1991.

Camille, Michael. "Seeing and Reading: Some Visual Implications of Medieval Literacy and Illiteracy." *Art History* 8.1 (1985): 26-49.

———. *The Gothic Idol: Ideology and Image-making in Medieval Art*. Cambridge: Cambridge UP, 1989.

———. "Philological Iconoclasm: Edition and Image in the *Vie de Saint Alexis*." *Medievalism and the Modernist Temper*. Ed. R. Howard Bloch and Stephen G. Nichols. Baltimore: The Johns Hopkins UP, 1996. 371-401.

Castro, Américo. *The Spaniards: An Introduction to their History*. Trans. Willard F. King and Selma Margaretten. Berkeley: U California P, 1971.

Cazelles, Brigitte. *The Lady as Saint: A Collection of French Hagiographic Romances of the Thirteenth Century*. Philadelphia: U Pennsylvania P, 1991.

———. "Introduction." Blumenfeld-Kosinski and Szell 1-17.

Copeland, Rita. *Rhetoric, Hermeneutics, and Translation in the Middle Ages: Academic traditions and vernacular texts*. Cambridge: Cambridge UP, 1991.

Corfis, Ivy A., ed. *Historia de la linda Melosina*. By Jean d'Arras. Madison: Hispanic Seminary of Medieval Studies, 1986.

Corominas, Joan. *Diccionario crítico etimológico de la lengua castellana*. Madrid: Gredos, 1955-57. 4 vols.

Crossan, John Dominic. *The Historical Jesus: The Life of a Mediterranean Jewish Peasant*. New York: HarperSanFrancisco, 1992.

———. *Jesus: A Revolutionary Biography*. San Francisco: HarperCollins, 1995.

Dagenais, John. "That Bothersome Residue: Toward a Theory of the Physical Text." *Vox intexta: Orality and Textuality in the Middle Ages*. Ed. A. N. Doane and Carol Braun Pasternack. Madison: U Wisconsin P, 1991. 246-262.

———. *The Ethics of Reading in Manuscript Culture: Glossing the "Libro de buen amor"*. Princeton: Princeton UP, 1994.

Delany, Sheila. Introduction. *A Legend of Holy Women: A translation of Osbern Bokenham's "Legends of Holy Women"*. Notre Dame, Indiana: U of Notre Dame P, 1992.

Deyermond, A. D. *The Middle Ages*. New York: Barnes and Noble, 1971. Vol. 1 of *A Literary History of Spain*. 8 vols.

Diccionario de historia eclesiástica de España. 4 vols. Dirigido por Quintín Aldea Vaquero, Tomás Marín Martínez and José Vives Gatell. Madrid: CSIC, 1975.

Fane, Diana, ed. *Converging Cultures: Art and Identity in Spanish America*. New York: Harry N. Abrams, 1996.

Finet-van der Schaaf, Baukje. "Le Roman en prose néerlandais de la reine Sibille et son modèle espagnol: *La Hystoria de la Reyna Sebilla*." *Charlemagne in the*

North. Ed. Philip E. Bennett, Anne Elizabeth Cobby, and Graham A. Runnalls. Edinburgh: Société Rencesvals British Branch, 1993. 31-43.

Ford, J. D. M. "The Saint's Life in Vernacular Literature of the Middle Ages." *The Catholic Historical Review* 17 (1931-32): 268-277.

Friedländer, Max J. *Lucas van Leyden and Other Dutch Masters of His Time*. Vol. 10 of *Early Netherlandish Painting*. tr. Heinz Norden. Leyden: A. W. Sijthoff, 1973.

Frugoni, Chiara. "The Imagined Woman." *Silences of the Middle Ages*. Ed. Christiane Klapsich-Zuber. Cambridge: Belknap P of Harvard UP, 1992, 336-422. Vol. 2 of *A History of Women in the West*. 3 vols.

Gardiner, F. C. *The Pilgrimage of Desire: A Study of Theme and Genre in Medieval Literature*. Leiden: E. J. Brill, 1971.

Gerli, E. Michael, ed. *Arcipreste de Talavera o Corbacho*. By Alfonso Martínez de Toledo. Madrid: Cátedra, 1987.

———. "La 'Religión del amor' y el antifeminismo en las letras castellanas del siglo XV." *Hispanic Review* 49 (1981): 65-86.

Goldberg, Harriet. "Sexual Humor in Misogynist Medieval Exempla." Miller 67-83.

———. "The Several Faces of Ugliness in Medieval Castilian Literature." *La Corónica* 7 (1979): 80-92.

González, Cristina. "*Otas* a la luz del folklore." *Romance Quarterly* 35.2 (1988): 179-191.

———. "*Vna santa enperatris*: novela esquizofrénica." *Homenatge a Josep Roca-Pons: Estudis de llengua i literatura*. Ed. Jane White Albrecht, Janet Ann De Cesaris, Patricia V. Junn and Josep Miquel Sobrer. Barcelona: Publicacions de l'Abadia de Montserrat and Indiana U, 1991: 153-165.

González Vázquez, Marta. *Las mujeres de la Edad Media y el Camino de Santiago*. Santiago: Xunta de Galicia, 1989.

Green, James Ray. Rev. of *"Carlos Maynes" and "La enperatrís de Roma": Critical Edition and Study of Two Medieval Spanish Romances*. Ed. Anita Benaim de Lasry. *Hispanic Review* 52 (1984): 527-529.

Gumpert Melgosa, Carlos. Rev. of *El Rey Guillelme*. Ed. John R. Maier. *El Crotalón: Anuario de Filología Española* 2 (1985): 581-587.

Gutiérrez, Gustavo. *Las Casas: In Search of the Poor of Jesus Christ*. Trans. Robert R. Barr. Maryknoll, New York: Orbis Books, 1993.

Haines, Victor Yelverton. *The Fortunate Fall of Sir Gawain: The Typology of "Sir Gawain and the Green Knight"*. Washington, D. C.: UP of America, 1982.

Hitt, Jack. *Off the Road: A Modern-Day Walk Down the Pilgrim's Road into Spain*. New York: Simon and Schuster, 1994.

Holloway, Julia Bolton. *The Pilgrim and the Book: A Study of Dante, Langland and Chaucer*. New York: Peter Lang, 1987.

Infantes, Víctor. "La narración caballeresca breve." *Evolución narrativa e ideológica de la literatura caballeresca*. Ed. María Eugenia Lacarra. Bilbao: Universidad del País Vasco, 1991. 165-181.

Kay, Sarah. *The 'Chansons de geste' in the Age of Romance*. Oxford: Clarendon P, 1995.

Kieckhefer, Richard. *Magic in the Middle Ages*. Cambridge: Cambridge UP, 1989.

Köhler, Reinhold. "Zu der altspanischen Erzählung von Karl dem Grossen und seiner Gemahlin Sibille." *Jahrbuch für Romanische und Englische Literatur* 12 (1871): 286-316.

Lacarra, María Jesús. *Cuentística medieval en España: los orígenes*. Zaragoza: Departamento de Literatura Española, Universidad de Zaragoza, n.d.

Ladner, Gerhart B. "*Homo Viator*: Mediaeval Ideas on Alienation and Order." *Speculum* 42 (1967): 233-259.

Liffen, Shirley. "The transformation of a *passio* into a romance: A study of two fourteenth-century Spanish versions of the legends of St Eustace and King William of England." *Iberoromania* 41 (1995): 1-16.

Maddox, Donald L. "Pilgrimage Narrative and Meaning in Manuscripts L and A of the *Vie de Saint Alexis.*" *Romance Philology* 27 (1973): 143-157.

Maier, John R. "Of Accused Queens and Wild Men: Folkloric Elements in Carlos Maynes." *La Corónica* 12 (1983): 21-31.

———. "Sainthood, Heroism, and Sexuality in the *Estoria de Santa Maria Egiçiaca.*" *Revista Canadiense de Estudios Hispánicos* 8 (1984): 424-435.

Maier, John R. and Thomas D. Spaccarelli. "MS. Escurialense h-I-13: Approaches to a Medieval Anthology." *La Corónica* 11 (1982): 18-34.

Melczer, William. *The Pilgrim's Guide to Santiago de Compostela.* New York: Italica P, 1993.

Menocal. María Rosa. *Shards of Love: Exile and the Origins of the Lyric.* Durham: Duke UP, 1994.

Michel, Sister Eleanore, ed. *"Vidas de Santa Maria Madalena y Santa Marta" an Edition of the Old Spanish Text.* Diss. U of Chicago, 1930.

Miller, Beth, ed. *Women in Hispanic Literature: Icons and Fallen Idols.* Berkeley: U California P, 1983.

Morrás, María. Rev. of *The Lives of St. Mary Magdalen and St. Martha.* Ed. John Rees-Smith. *La Corónica* 21 (1992-93): 115-121.

Morreale, Margherita. Rev. of *Estoria de Santa Maria Egiçiaca.* Ed. Roger M. Walker. *Zeitschrift für Romansche Philologie* 90 (1974): 400-404.

Muriel Tapia, María Cruz. *Antifeminismo y subestimación de la mujer en la literatura medieval castellana.* Cáceres: Editorial Guadiloba, 1991.

Nichols, Stephen G., Jr. *Romanesque Signs: Early Medieval Narrative and Iconography.* New Haven: Yale UP, 1983.

Nouwen, Henri J. M. *Reaching Out: The Three Movements of the Spiritual Life.* Garden City, N. Y.: Doubleday, 1975.

Nunes, José Joaquim. *Crestomatia Arcaica: Excertos da Literatura Portuguesa.* Lisboa: A. M. Teixeira, 1976.

Ong, Walter J. "Orality, Literacy, and Medieval Textualization." *New Literary History* 16.1 (1984-85): 1-12.

Ornstein, Jacob. "La misoginia y el profeminismo en la literatura castellana." *Revista de Filología Hispánica* 3 (1941): 219-232.

Palmer, Parker J. *The Company of Strangers: Christians and the Renewal of America's Public Life.* New York: Crossroads, 1983.

Pérez de Urbel, Justo. *El monasterio en la vida española de la Edad Media.* Barcelona: Editorial Labor, 1942.

———. *El claustro de Silos.* Third ed. Burgos: Ediciones de la Institución Fernán González, 1975.

Perry, Mary Elizabeth. *Gender and Disorder in Early Modern Seville.* Princeton: Princeton UP, 1990.

Rees Smith, John, ed. *The Lives of St Mary Magdalene and St Martha (MS Esc. h-I-13).* Exeter: U of Exeter P, 1989.

Rincón García, Wifredo. "Aproximación a la iconografía de dos santos del Camino de Santiago: Santo Domingo de la Calzada y San Juan de Ortega." Santiago-Otero 221-228.

Robertson, Elizabeth. "The Corporeality of Female Sanctity in *The Life of Saint Margaret.*" Blumenfeld-Kosinski and Szell 268-287.

Santiago-Otero, Horacio, coordinador. *El Camino de Santiago, la hospitalidad monástica y las peregrinaciones.* Salamanca: Junta de Castilla y León, 1992.

Schlauch, Margaret. *Chaucer's Constance and Accused Queens.* New York: New York UP, 1927.

Shaver-Crandell, Annie and Paula Gerson. *The Pilgrim's Guide to Santiago de Compostela: A Gazateer*. London: Harvey Miller, 1995.

Smith, C. C. "On the Ethos of the 'Romancero viejo'." *Studies of the Spanish and Portuguese Ballad*. Ed. N. D. Shergold. London: Tamesis, 1972. 5-24.

Snow, Joseph T. "Notes on the Fourteenth-Century Spanish Translation of Paul the Deacon's *Vita Sanctae Mariae Aegyptiacae, Meretricis*." *Saints and their Authors: Studies in Medieval Hispanic Hagiography in Honor of John K. Walsh*. Ed. Jane E. Connolly, Alan Deyermond, Brian Dutton. Madison: Hispanic Seminary of Medieval Studies, 1990. 83-96.

Spaccarelli, Thomas D. Rev. of *"Carlos Maynes" and "La enperatrís de Roma": Critical Edition and Study of Two Medieval Spanish Romances*. Ed. Anita Benaim de Lasry. *Journal of Hispanic Philology* 8 (1982): 61-65.

———. "A Wasteland of Textual Criticism: A Note on Paleography in the *Noble cuento del enperador Carlos Maynes*." *Romance Notes* 25 (1984): 193-198.

———. "The Symbolic Substructure of the *Noble cuento del enperador Carlos Maynes*." *Hispanófila* 89 (1987): 1-19.

———. "Recovering the Lost Folios of the *Noble cuento del enperador Carlos Maynes*: the Restoration of a Medieval Anthology." *Romance Quarterly* 43 (1996): 217-233.

Starkie, Walter. *The Road to Santiago: Pilgrims of St. James*. Berkeley: U California P, 1965.

Stock, Brian. *The Implications of Literacy: Written Language and Models of Interpretation in the Eleventh and Twelfth Centuries*. Princeton: Princeton UP, 1983.

———. "Medieval Literacy, Linguistic Theory, and Social Organization." *New Literary History* 16.1 (1984-85): 13-29.

Suárez González, Ana. "La hospitalidad en San Isidoro de León según los manuscritos de su archivo (siglos XII-XIII)." Santiago-Otero 53-61.

Sumption, Jonathan. *Pilgrimage: An Image of Mediaeval Religion*. London: Faber and Faber, 1975.

Turner, Victor. *Process, Performance and Pilgrimage: A Study in Comparative Symbology*. New Delhi: Concept Publishing Co., 1979.

Uitti, Karl D. "Women Saints, the Vernacular, and History in Early Medieval France." Blumenfeld-Kosinski and Szell 247-267.

Vauchez, André. "Lay People's Sanctity in Western Europe: Evolution of a Pattern (Twelfth and Thirteenth Centuries)." Blumenfeld-Kosinski and Szell 21-32.

Vázquez de Parga, Luis, José María Lacarra and Juan Uría Riu. *Las peregrinaciones a Santiago de Compostela*. 3 vols. Madrid: Consejo Superior de Investigaciones Científicas, 1949.

Viñayo González, Antonio. "La hospitalidad monástica en las Reglas de San Isidoro de Sevilla y San Fructuoso del Bierzo." Santiago-Otero 39-52.

Vitz, Evelyn Birge. "From the Oral to the Written in Medieval and Renaissance Saints' Lives." Blumenfeld-Kosinski and Szell 97-114.

Walker, Roger M. "Oral Delivery or Private Reading? A Contribution to the Debate on the Dissemination of Medieval Literature." *Forum for Modern Language Studies* 7 (1971): 36-42.

———. "A Possible Source for the 'Arfrenta de Corpes' Episode in the 'Poema de Mio Cid'" *Modern Language Review* 72 (1977): 335-347.

———. "From French Verse to Spanish Prose: *La Chanson de Florence de Rome* and *El cuento del enperador Otas de Roma*." *Medium Aevum* 49.2 (1980): 230-243.

———. Rev. of *"Carlos Maynes" and "La enperatrís de Roma": Critical Edition and Study of Two Medieval Spanish Romances*. Ed. Anita Benaim de Lasry. *La Corónica* 13 (1984): 298-301.

Walsh, John K. "The Chivalric Dragon: Hagiographic Parallels in Early Spanish Romances." *Bulletin of Hispanic Studies* 54 (1977): 189-198.

————. *Relic and Literature: St Toribius of Astorga and his "Arca Sancta"*, ed. by Alan Deyermond and Billy Bussell Thompson. Fontaine Notre Dame Series 2. St. Albans: David Hook, 1992.

Walsh, J. K. and B. Bussell Thompson, eds. *The Myth of the Magdalen in Early Spanish Literature (with an edition of the Vida de Santa Maria Madalena in MS. h-I-13 of the Escorial Library)*. New York: Lorenzo Clemente, 1986.

Wardropper, Bruce W. "*El Burlador de Sevilla*: A Tragedy of Errors." *Philological Quarterly* 36 (1957): 61-71.

Whinnom, Keith. *Spanish Literary Historiography: Three Forms of Distortion*. Exeter, 1967.

Williams, Edwin B. *From Latin to Portuguese*. Philadelphia: U of Pennsylvania P, 1962.

Zumthor, Paul. "The Text and the Voice." *New Literary History* 16.1 (1984-85): 67-92.

NORTH CAROLINA STUDIES IN THE ROMANCE LANGUAGES AND LITERATURES

I.S.B.N. Prefix 0-8078-

Recent Titles

When ordering please cite the *ISBN Prefix* plus the last four digits for each title.

Send orders to: University of North Carolina Press
P.O. Box 2288
CB# 6215
Chapel Hill, NC 27515-2288
U.S.A.